THE OFFICIAL
MANCHESTER
UNITED
BOOK OF FACTS AND FIGURES

ABOUT THE AUTHOR

Born in Lancashire in 1966, Ian Marshall is a lifelong Red who first went to Old Trafford to see United play in 1973. After graduating from Durham University, he worked in book publishing for many years and published the autobiographies of Eric Cantona and Lee Sharpe among many others. He is the author of the *Playfair Cricket Annual*, the world's bestselling cricket yearbook, and *Old Trafford: The Official Story of the Home of Manchester United*. He now lives in Eastbourne, with his wife and two young daughters.

THE OFFICIAL
MANCHESTER
UNITED
BOOK OF FACTS AND FIGURES

IAN MARSHALL

**SIMON &
SCHUSTER**

London · New York · Sydney · Toronto · New Delhi

A CBS COMPANY

To Sugra, with all my love

First published in Great Britain by Simon & Schuster UK Ltd, 2011
A CBS COMPANY

1 3 5 7 9 10 8 6 4 2

Simon & Schuster UK Ltd
1st Floor
222 Gray's Inn Road
London
WC1X 8HB

www.simonandschuster.co.uk

Simon & Schuster Australia, Sydney
Simon & Schuster India, New Delhi

A CIP catalogue for this book is available
from the British Library.

ISBN: 978-1-84737-920-7

Typeset by M Rules
Printed and bound by CPI Group (UK) Ltd, Croydon, CR0 4YY

CONTENTS

INTRODUCTION

There are certain facts that everyone knows about Manchester United – that in 2011 they became league champions for a record 19th time, for example. We also know that Ryan Giggs has made a record number of appearances for the Reds, dating back more than 20 years. Fans remember that no one has scored more goals for the club than Sir Bobby Charlton. And all United fans are delighted that no manager in the history of the game has won more trophies than Sir Alex Ferguson.

But what about those who just missed out on setting a club record? Or those players who have made their mark in some smaller way on Old Trafford's history? For example: who was the first substitute ever used by United? Which future cricket Test match umpire once scored against the Reds? Who were the ten goalkeepers used by United between the departure of Peter Schmeichel and the arrival of Edwin van der Sar?

The answers to all these questions, and many more, can be found within these pages. It has been great fun researching the lists compiled here, helping me to relive great goals, games and players from the past. In researching the lists contained in this book, I have tried to tell as much of United's incredible story as possible, expanding upon one of the entries in each list to fill in the background. I've not always chosen the one at the top of the list, either, as sometimes the more interesting story comes lower down the rankings. All those players who have made a truly significant impact on the club should be featured somewhere within these pages. The only player not to be profiled from the all-time Top 30 list of appearances made or goals scored made his debut way back in 1893.

It would not have been possible to write and research this book without access to the club's wonderful statistics website, www. stretfordend. co.uk, run by Andrew Endlar. All United statistics in this book are taken from these official figures. Statistics from beyond the club are usually based on those found in the *Sky Sports Football Yearbook* (Headline), which has been lovingly compiled for many years now by Jack and Glenda Rollin.

I would also like to thank Gary Neville and Chris Smalling for providing their own personal lists, which I hope give an insight into their thoughts and, indeed, those they most admire. Thanks to Steve Bartram and Gemma Thompson for putting their words down on paper, and to James White for helping make this happen (and for all his other assistance). My thanks go to Mark Wylie, curator of the Old Trafford museum, who was also a valuable source of knowledge and help; to Jack Rollin; Rhea Halford and John English, who read the manuscript and proofs, and made many helpful suggestions, spotting various errors. Of course, any errors or omissions in this book are mine, not theirs.

Ian Marshall
Eastbourne, July 2011

All facts and figures in this book are correct to 1 August 2011.

LIST OF ABBREVIATIONS USED

1, 2, etc.	Round	Gp	Group stage
CL	Champions League	ICFC	Inter-Cities' Fairs Cup
CS	Charity/Community Shield	LC	League Cup
		PL	Premier League
Div 1	First Division	Pr	Preliminary round
Div 2	Second Division	Q	Qualifying round
EC	European Cup	QF	Quarter-final
ECWC	European Cup-Winners' Cup	R	Replay
		SF	Semi-final
F	Final	UEFA	UEFA Cup
FAC	FA Cup		

NB. Throughout the book, for convenience I have used the most recent competition titles to denote various tournaments, so 'Champions League' refers to both the Champions League and its forerunner the European Cup, while Europa League refers to its various predecessors, such as the UEFA Cup and the Inter-Cities' Fairs Cup. However, the Premier League (which began in 1992-93) is treated separately to the old First Division.

'Career' in the list headings refers to the period of time from when a player made his first-team debut to the date of his last game for United, unless otherwise specified. 'Appearances' includes substitute appearances, unless they are separately listed. Appearance totals include all games played in league football, the FA Cup, League Cup, European Cup/Champions League, UEFA Cup (in its various guises), European Cup-Winners' Cup; the club also deems appearances in 'Test Matches', Charity/Community Shield and various one-off trophies, such as the Inter-continental cup, UEFA Super Cup and so on to count towards the total; some sources do not include these figures, which may explain any discrepancies in figures.

MOST APPEARANCES IN A CAREER

	Player	Career	Appearances
1	Ryan Giggs	1991–	876
2	Bobby Charlton	1956–73	758
3	**Bill Foulkes**	**1952–69**	**688**
4	Paul Scholes	1994–2011	676
5	Gary Neville	1992–2011	602
6	Alex Stepney	1966–78	539
7	Tony Dunne	1960–73	535
8	Denis Irwin	1990–2002	529
9	Joe Spence	1919–33	510
10	Arthur Albiston	1974–88	485

When Bill Foulkes retired after 17 years at United, he easily held the record for the most appearances made in the club's first 90 years or so. He came from a rugby-playing family in St Helens and was working for the coal board there when he was spotted by a United scout. For someone who was known as a resolute defender, it will surprise many to learn that he was signed up as a forward, and was due to make his first-team debut up front. But an ankle injury robbed him of his chance, and when he did eventually pull on the famous red shirt, it was as a defender. Indeed, he was still in a great deal of pain when he had to prove his fitness – by jumping up and down in Matt Busby's office! In his long and distinguished career, he won four league titles (a club record that lasted until the 1990s), the FA Cup and the European Cup. He said his two toughest opponents were Florian Albert of Ferencvaros and Alfredo di Stefano of Real Madrid.

MOST GOALS IN THE PREMIER LEAGUE

	Player	PL Career	Appearances	Goals
1	Ryan Giggs	1992–	573	105
2	Paul Scholes	1994–2011	466	102
2	Wayne Rooney	2004–	217	102
4	Ruud van Nistelrooy	2001–06	150	95
5	Andrew Cole	1995–2001	195	93
6	Ole Gunnar Solskjaer	1996–2007	235	91
7	Cristiano Ronaldo	2003–09	196	84
8	Eric Cantona	1992–97	143	64
9	David Beckham	1995–2003	265	62
10	Dwight Yorke	1998–2002	96	48

Recognised by many as the finest midfielder of the Premier League era, Paul Scholes began banging in the goals for United in 1994, and continued for 17 successive seasons. His first came against Ipswich Town at Portman Road on 24 September 1994, but wasn't enough to prevent the Reds going down to a 3–2 defeat. The following season, as United went on to achieve their second Double, he hit ten in the Premier League, but his most prolific campaign came in 2002–03 when he scored 14 times. That season he was often used as an auxiliary striker, operating behind Ruud van Nistelrooy, and it was at St James' Park on 12 April that he hit his second Premier League hat-trick, all three goals scored in 18 minutes either side of half-time as part of a stunning all-round performance. Before the game, one of the Newcastle players had questioned the view that Scholes should be an automatic England pick. This was the devastating response from the Salford-born ginger maestro – as all United fans know: he scores goals.

BIGGEST WINS IN THE PREMIER LEAGUE

	Opposition	Venue	Date	Score
1	Ipswich Town	Old Trafford	4 March 1995	9–0
2	Nottingham Forest	City Ground	6 February 1999	8–1
3	Barnsley	Old Trafford	25 October 1997	7–0
4	West Ham United	Old Trafford	1 April 2000	7–1
4	Blackburn Rovers	Old Trafford	27 November 2010	7–1
6	Bolton Wanderers	Burnden Park	25 February 1996	6–0
6	Bradford City	Old Trafford	5 September 2000	6–0
6	Newcastle United	Old Trafford	12 January 2008	6–0
9	Sheffield Wednesday	Old Trafford	1 November 1997	6–1
9	Arsenal	Old Trafford	25 February 2001	6–1
9	Southampton	Old Trafford	22 December 2001	6–1

United's remarkable triumph over Ipswich remains the joint-biggest victory in Premier League history. The hero was new signing Andrew Cole, who had recently joined United for a record deal valued at £7 million. He had made his debut on 22 January, and had already scored twice. But it was this game that showed exactly what he was: a lethal predator in the box. He played 275 times for United, scoring 121 goals; on five occasions, he scored a hat-trick or better. No one has yet bettered his record of five goals in a Premier League game, though Alan Shearer, Jermain Defoe and Dimitar Berbatov (v Blackburn, above) have since equalled his feat. The other scorers that day were Mark Hughes (two), Roy Keane and Paul Ince. According to Alex Ferguson, United's performance that day 'could have been set to music'. However, despite the win, United remained three points behind Blackburn Rovers in the race for the title and eventually missed out by just one point.

MOST APPEARANCES FOR UNITED BY SCOTTISH PLAYERS

	Player	Career	Appearances
1	Arthur Albiston	1974–88	485
2	Brian McClair	1987–98	471
3	Martin Buchan	1972–82	456
4	Denis Law	1962–73	404
5	Lou Macari	1973–84	401
6	Pat Crerand	1963–71	397
7	Fred Erentz	1892–1902	310
8	Alex Bell	1903–13	309
9	Willie Morgan	1968–75	296
10	Darren Fletcher	2003–	292

When Arthur Albiston was selected as left-back for the FA Cup final of 1977 against champions Liverpool, he was still only 19 and had started fewer than 30 games for United. With regular full-back Stewart Houston out injured, it was a high-risk strategy by manager Tommy Docherty, but the youngster handled the occasion superbly and helped the team to a 2–1 victory. Born in Edinburgh, he had joined the club as an apprentice and was still going strong more than a decade later in the early days of the Ferguson era, by which stage he was the longest-serving player. He is the only Scot in United's Top 10 appearance makers. He played for a variety of clubs after leaving United, including Norwegian side Molde, whom he left just before a certain Ole Gunnar Solskjaer arrived. He won 14 caps for Scotland, making his debut against Northern Ireland in April 1982 and concluding his international career (like Denis Law before him) with his only World Cup appearance – a 0–0 draw against Uruguay in 1986. He now works on MUTV as a pundit.

MOST GOALS FOR UNITED BY SCOTTISH PLAYERS

	Player	Career	Goals
1	Denis Law	1962–73	237
2	**David Herd**	**1961–68**	**145**
3	Brian McClair	1987–98	127
4	Sandy Turnbull	1907–15	101
5	Joe Cassidy	1893–1900	100
6	Lou Macari	1973–84	97
7	Tom Reid	1929–33	67
8	Bob Donaldson	1892–97	66
9	Jack Peddie	1902–07	58
10	Alex Dawson	1957–61	54★

In the 1960s title-winning sides of 1965 and 1967, much of the glory went to the combination of Best, Charlton and Law, but David Herd was a vital part of the attacking threat. He was signed from Arsenal in summer 1961 for a fee of £35,000. In his six full seasons at Old Trafford, he was never once out of the top two in the scoring charts, proving an ideal partner for Law. He first tasted glory in the 1963 FA Cup final, when he scored twice (both from rebounds off Leicester keeper Gordon Banks) in United's 3–1 win. Although not great in the air, he had a powerful shot. Often under-rated by the fans, though not by his team-mates, the Hamilton-born forward was also overlooked by Scotland's selectors, never playing for his country while at United, despite having previously won five caps, scoring three times. It was a curious omission as he was one of the most consistent performers at that time, before a broken leg curtailed his career.

★NB. Although Dawson played for England Schoolboys, he was born in Aberdeen and considers himself Scottish.

CHRIS SMALLING'S TOP 10 DEFENDERS

	Player	Main Teams
1	Tony Adams	Arsenal and England
2	Roberto Carlos	Inter Milan, Real Madrid, Fenerbahce and Brazil
3	Patrice Evra	Nice, Monaco, Manchester United and France
4	Rio Ferdinand	West Ham, Leeds, Manchester United and England
5	Lucio	Bayer Leverkusen, Bayern Munich, Inter Milan and Brazil
6	Maicon	Monaco, Inter and Brazil
7	Alessandro Nesta	Lazio, AC Milan and Italy
8	Carles Puyol	Barcelona and Spain
9	John Terry	Chelsea and England
10	Nemanja Vidic	Red Star Belgrade, Manchester United and Serbia

Chris Smalling joined United from Fulham at the start of the 2010–11 season and picked his Top 10 defenders, in alphabetical order, commenting: 'There are so many great defenders I look up to. Growing up, Tony Adams was someone who I watched a lot of. He had such a great attitude and determination and gave everything for the cause. He's like Vida [Nemanja Vidic] in that sense, and both have been massive leaders for club and country. Some people have compared me to Rio, which is a real compliment. Even before I joined the club, I watched him a lot for both United and England. He is definitely someone any young centre-back should look up to if they want to become a top player. He's one of England's greatest ever defenders. Both he and Vida have already given me a lot of advice and confidence. I'm lucky to play alongside a host of top players at United and all the opportunities I get to train and play with them will only help me improve.'

LEAST PROLIFIC GOALSCORERS

	Player	Career	Goals	Appearances	Strike Rate*
1	Tony Dunne	1960–73	2	535	0.37
2	Jack Silcock	1919–34	2	449	0.45
3	George Vose	1933–38	1	209	0.48
4	Harry Stafford	1896–1903	1	200	0.50
5	Jack Griffiths	1934–39	1	173	0.58
6	Allenby Chilton	1946–55	3	391	0.77
7	Jaap Stam	1998–2001	1	127	0.79
8	Mark Jones	1950–58	1	121	0.83
9	Martin Buchan	1972–82	4	456	0.88
10	James Brown	1935–39	1	110	0.91
10	Graeme Hogg	1984–88	1	110	0.91

Of all the outfield players ever to score for United, Tony Dunne was the one least likely to do so. His two goals came in a 3–3 draw away against West Bromwich Albion on 4 May 1966 and in a 2–2 draw away to Newcastle United on 9 December 1967, both in the league. Dunne was a pacy left-back signed from Shelbourne for just £5,000 in 1960 and eventually succeeded Noel Cantwell in that role. Like fellow Irishman Denis Irwin in a later era, he was an unsung hero in a side full of stars, helping United to win the European Cup in 1968. In 1964–65, he played in all 60 of United's fixtures as they won the league title, which was typical of his consistency. Soon after Tommy Docherty arrived as manager in December 1972, he was sold to Bolton Wanderers. The fact that he went on to make another 200 appearances for them shows how much more he still had to give.

*Goals per 100 games.

MOST APPEARANCES BY
MATT BUSBY'S SIGNINGS

	Player	Career	Appearances	Goals
1	Alex Stepney	1966–78	539	2
2	Tony Dunne	1960–73	535	2
3	Denis Law	1962–73	404	237
4	Pat Crerand	1963–71	397	15
5	David Sadler	1963–73	335	27
6	Willie Morgan	1968–75	296	34
7	Johnny Berry	1951–57	276	45
8	David Herd	1961–68	265	145
9	Harry Gregg	1957–66	247	0
10	Ray Wood	1949–58	208	0

Matt Busby's signing of Alex Stepney from Chelsea for a world record fee for a keeper of £55,000 in September 1966 solved a problem for United. Since 1959–60, only once had the Reds had a keeper play 30-plus league games in a season, and that time (1964–65) they won the title. In Stepney, they had a keeper of the utmost consistency and reliability, missing just ten league games in his first four seasons. He brought reassurance to the defence, helping them to the title in his first campaign and then to the European Cup in 1968. Faced with the great Eusebio of Benfica bearing down on him in the dying moments of the final, he made a terrific save that ensured the game went to extra time, where United won 4–1 (he modestly states: 'Actually he hit it straight at me.'). He was a regular between the posts for a further decade, adding the FA Cup winner's medal to his collection in 1977, before eventually leaving the club at the end of the following season. His two goals came in 1973–74, when he was United's penalty-taker – for a while he was the joint top scorer.

FIRST WORLD CUP GOALSCORERS*

	Player	Team	Opposition	Date
1	Bobby Charlton	England	Argentina	2 June 1962
2	Bobby Charlton	England	Mexico	16 July 1966
3	Bobby Charlton	England	Portugal	26 July 1966
4	Bobby Charlton	England	Portugal	26 July 1966
5	Joe Jordan	Scotland	Peru	3 June 1978
6	Bryan Robson	England	France	16 June 1982
7	Bryan Robson	England	France	16 June 1982
8	Norman Whiteside	N. Ireland	Algeria	3 June 1986
9	Gordon Strachan	Scotland	West Germany	8 June 1986

With the physique of Duncan Edwards and the background of George Best, Norman Whiteside was another teenage sensation to make an instant impact at Old Trafford. His goal in the 1986 World Cup came in his second tournament, as he had appeared in the 1982 finals for Northern Ireland at the age of 17 years and 41 days, breaking Pelé's record. At that stage, he had appeared just twice for United, making his debut as a 16-year-old substitute against Brighton on 24 April. For the final game of the season, he started – and scored a goal, aged 17 years and 8 days (a club record). The following season, he scored in both the League Cup final (which United lost) and the FA Cup final replay, where Brighton were thumped 4–0. He therefore became the youngest to score in the finals of both competitions. Having started as a striker, he moved increasingly to fill a midfield role and was equally effective in either position. Had a long-standing knee injury not brought his career to an end at 26, it is certain he would have achieved even more.

*James Brown, who played for United between 1932 and 1934, scored a goal for the USA in the 1930 World Cup semi-final.

ENGLISH OPPONENTS IN EUROPEAN COMPETITIONS

	Opponents	Venue	Date	Competition	Score
1	Tottenham Hotspur	Away	3 December 1963	ECWC 2	0–2
2	Tottenham Hotspur	Home	10 December 1963	ECWC 2	4–1
3	Everton	Home	20 January 1965	ICFC 3	1–1
4	Everton	Away	9 February 1965	ICFC 3	2–1
5	Chelsea	Neutral	21 May 2008	CL F	1–1
6	Arsenal	Home	29 April 2009	CL SF	1–0
7	Arsenal	Away	5 May 2009	CL SF	3–1
8	Chelsea	Away	6 April 2011	CL QF	1–0
9	Chelsea	Home	12 April 2011	CL QF	2–1

On the five occasions to date that United have been drawn against English opposition in European competition, each time the Reds have won through. But no meeting was quite so important as the Champions League final in 2008. Inspired by Cristiano Ronaldo, who scored 42 goals that campaign, United had finished the season as Premier League champions and were looking to add European success as well. Almost inevitably, it was Ronaldo who gave United the lead in Moscow with a towering header on 26 minutes, only for Chelsea to equalise just before half-time. Thereafter, there were no more goals in normal time, nor in the 30 minutes of extra time, so it came down to penalties. Carlos Tevez and Michael Carrick scored theirs before Ronaldo's shot was saved. Owen Hargreaves and Nani kept United in it, and Chelsea captain John Terry hit the post with his. Sudden death and first Anderson then Ryan Giggs scored, before Edwin van der Sar saved from Nicolas Anelka to ensure United were champions of Europe for a third time.

NB: United also played Wrexham in the 1990–91 European Cup-Winners' Cup, but although they play in the Football League, they had qualified as winners of the Welsh Cup.

UNITED'S FIRST SUBSTITUTES★

	Player	Opponent	Date	Score
1	John Fitzpatrick	Tottenham Hotspur	16 October 1965	1–5
2	John Connelly	Blackburn Rovers	6 November 1965	2–2
3	David Herd	West Ham United	30 April 1966	2–3
4	Willie Anderson	West Bromwich Albion	4 May 1966	3–3
5	John Aston Jr	Tottenham Hotspur	10 September 1966	2–1
6	John Aston Jr	Burnley	24 September 1966	4–1
7	John Aston Jr	Sheffield Wednesday	12 November 1966	2–0
8	John Aston Jr	Southampton	19 November 1966	2–1
9	Willie Anderson	Liverpool	10 December 1966	2–2
10	Jimmy Ryan	Nottingham Forest	11 February 1967	1–0
11	David Sadler (1 goal)	Leicester City	18 March 1967	5–2

In the first two seasons that substitutes were allowed in English league football, Matt Busby turned to the bench on just 11 occasions, and only once did the fresh player score. David Sadler was part of the famous Youth Cup-winning side of 1964, along with Willie Anderson, John Aston and John Fitzpatrick – not to mention his great friend George Best, with whom he shared digs at Mrs Fullaway's house in their early days at the club. But, Best apart, it was Sadler who went on to have the most significant career at United, with his record as the scorer of the Reds' first substitute goal being a statistical footnote. In his early days, Sadler was a centre-forward, making his first-team debut in place of David Herd in August 1963. But on a summer tour in 1964, he was asked to step in at centre-half, and eventually played most of his career there, with the highlight being his appearance in the European Cup final of 1968.

★David Gaskell, who was in the crowd, came on as a substitute in the 1956 Charity Shield after United's first-choice keeper was injured during the match, but he was not originally named as a substitute.

BIGGEST WINS AGAINST LIVERPOOL

	Date	Venue	Score	Scorers
1	5 May 1928	Old Trafford	6–1	Spence 3, Rawlings 2, Hanson
2	11 September 1946	Maine Road	5–0	Pearson 3, Mitten, Rowley
3	19 December 1953	Old Trafford	5–1	Blanchflower 2, Taylor 2, Viollet
4	7 September 1907	Bank Street	4–0	A.Turnbull 3, Wall
4	12 April 1952	Old Trafford	4–0	Byrne 2, Downie, Rowley
4	**5 April 2003**	**Old Trafford**	**4–0**	**Van Nistelrooy 2, Giggs, Solskjaer**
7	2 November 1895	Bank Street	5–2	Peters 3, Clarkin, Smith
8	6 April 1931	Old Trafford	4–1	Reid 2, McLenahan, Rowley
8	13 December 1969	Anfield	4–1	Charlton, Morgan, Ure, o.g.
10	1 November 1913	Old Trafford	3–0	Wall 2, West
10	24 January 1948	Goodison Park	3–0	Mitten, Morris, Rowley
10	23 March 2008	Old Trafford	3–0	Brown, Nani, Ronaldo

If there is one opponent that United fans want to beat possibly even more than Manchester City, it is Liverpool. When Alex Ferguson joined the club, he knew there was one side he had to 'knock off their perch' – the men from Anfield. The biggest win in his era came in 2002–03 when United were pushing to make up lost ground as they searched for an eighth Premiership title. Unbeaten since Boxing Day, this 4–0 triumph sent out a clear message to their rivals that they were not to be stopped. Ruud van Nistelrooy opened the scoring after just five minutes when he converted a penalty, after Sami Hyypia was sent off for pulling down the Dutchman as he ran on to Paul Scholes' pass. He scored another penalty midway through the second half, before Ryan Giggs and Ole Gunnar Solskjaer added two late goals against a tiring Merseyside outfit.

DOUBLE WINNERS

	Club	Season	League Runners-up	FA Cup Finalists
1	Preston North End	1888–89	Everton	Wolverhampton W
2	Aston Villa	1896–97	Sheffield United	Everton
3	Tottenham Hotspur	1960–61	Sheffield Wednesday	Leicester City
4	Arsenal	1970–71	Leeds United	Liverpool
5	Liverpool	1985–86	Everton	Everton
6	**Manchester United**	**1993–94**	**Blackburn Rovers**	**Chelsea**
7	Manchester United	1995–96	Newcastle United	Liverpool
8	Arsenal	1997–98	Manchester United	Newcastle United
9	Manchester United	1998–99	Arsenal	Newcastle United
10	Arsenal	2001–02	Liverpool	Chelsea
11	Chelsea	2009–10	Manchester United	Portsmouth

United's first Double was not only special in itself, it was the closest any team has ever come to completing the domestic Treble, as the Reds lost 3–1 to Aston Villa in the League Cup final. The Premier League title was secured on 2 May, the day after United had beaten Ipswich away. That game had proved a struggle – and costly, as Peter Schmeichel picked up an ankle ligament injury that threatened to keep him out of the FA Cup final. Ipswich took the lead midway through the first half, before Eric Cantona headed home an Andrei Kanchelskis cross. Then, just after the interval, Ryan Giggs finished from close range. The following day nearest rivals Blackburn lost at Coventry – and United were champions for a second successive season. Chelsea were thumped 4–0 in the FA Cup final, but it had needed a stunning Mark Hughes goal 81 seconds from the end of extra time in the semi-final against Oldham to keep their cup run going and arguably save the season.

MOST APPEARANCES IN THE FA CUP

	Player	Career	Appearances
1	Bobby Charlton	1956–73	78
2	Ryan Giggs	1991–	68
3	Bill Foulkes	1952–69	61
4	Tony Dunne	1960–73	55
5	Gary Neville	1992–2011	47
6	George Best	1963–74	46
6	Denis Law	1962–73	46
6	Mark Hughes	1983–95	46
6	Roy Keane	1993–2005	46
10	Brian McClair	1987–98	45

Bill Foulkes is one of only four men to have made more than 50 FA Cup appearances for United, three of which were Wembley finals, in 1957, 1958 and 1963. Having lost the first two finals, he was delighted to beat Leicester City 3–1 to make it third time lucky. But despite picking up a winner's medal then, there is little doubt which was the most significant of all his FA Cup appearances: the fifth-round tie against Sheffield Wednesday on 19 February 1958 – just 13 days after he survived the Munich Air Disaster. On a night of huge emotion at Old Trafford, he and goalkeeper Harry Gregg were the only two who had escaped from the wreckage of the plane that were able to play. Somehow, backed by a nation willing them on, the mixture of reserves and new signings combined to beat Wednesday 3–0. A full-back or more often centre-half, Foulkes was a strong and determined defender who gave no quarter. His intensity made him the perfect man to protect United's honour by keeping a clean sheet.

HAT-TRICKS IN THE FA CUP★

	Player	Opposition	Round	Date
1	Stan Pearson	Derby County	SF	13 March 1948
2	Jack Rowley (5)	Yeovil	5th	12 February 1949
3	Dennis Viollet	Workington	3rd	4 January 1958
4	Alex Dawson	Fulham	SF R	26 March 1958
5	Denis Law	Huddersfield Town	3rd	4 March 1963
6	Denis Law	Bristol Rovers	4th	25 January 1964
7	Denis Law	Sunderland	6th 2R	9 March 1964
8	Denis Law	Birmingham City	5th R	24 February 1969
9	George Best (6)	Northampton Town	5th	7 February 1970
10	Norman Whiteside	West Ham United	6th	9 March 1985

Since the war, United have a better record in the FA Cup than anyone, but there has been just one hat-trick for the Reds in the tournament since George Best's incredible performance against Northampton Town. One of only two men ever to have scored six times in a match for United (Harold Halse in the 1911 Charity Shield is the other), once again Best wrote the newspaper headlines for them: 'Six Of The Best' was inevitable. Best was just returning from a month's suspension when he lined up at the County Ground in front of 21,771 fans, many wondering if there might be an upset. Best headed home United's first midway through the first half, and quickly followed it up with a second. He completed his hat-trick soon after the break, before going on to claim a second hat-trick, and even set up Brian Kidd as United won 8–2. It was a stunning performance by the man rated by many to be the greatest ever to pull on the Red shirt for United.

★Since the Second World War.

UNITED'S NON-EUROPEAN OPPONENTS

	Opponents	Competition	Result	Date
1	Estudiantes	Inter-Continental Cup	0–1	25 September 1968
2	Estudiantes	Inter-Continental Cup	1–1	16 October 1968
3	Palmeiras	Inter-Continental Cup	1–0	30 November 1999
4	Club Necaxa	Club World Championship	1–1	6 January 2000
5	Vasco da Gama	Club World Championship	1–3	8 January 2000
6	South Melbourne	Club World Championship	2–0	11 January 2000
7	Gamba Osaka	Club World Cup	5–3	18 December 2008
8	Liga de Quito	Club World Cup	1–0	21 December 2008

Following United's three European Cup/Champions League triumphs in 1968, 1999 and 2008, the Reds have been involved in various tournaments to decide who is the 'best club in the world'. The first of these occasions was the most notorious, when United took on the Argentinian side Estudiantes de la Plata. Coming so soon after the 1966 World Cup, when Nobby Stiles had been such a controversial figure in England's game against Argentina, the Reds were never going to get a warm welcome in Buenos Aires. Even so, the match there was a disgrace, with Stiles sent off for retaliating after he had been headbutted. For the return leg, United looked to overturn a 1–0 deficit, but fell behind early on. A hostile crowd of 63,500 wanted revenge for the first leg, and bayed for blood every time a challenge, fair or foul, came in from Estudiantes. Willie Morgan equalised late on; George Best was sent off, having been constantly provoked throughout the game. As a last injustice, the referee blew the final whistle as the ball was en route to the back of the net. Perhaps it was just as well, as there would have been a replay if the aggregate scores had been equal.

TEN ONE-GOAL WONDERS

	Player	Opposition	Date
1	Harry Stafford	Portsmouth (H)	5 January 1901
2	Albert Kinsey	Chester (H)	9 January 1965
3	Laurie Cunningham	Watford (H)	23 April 1983
4	Peter Schmeichel	Rotor Volgograd (H)	26 September 1995
5	Terry Cooke	York City (A)	3 October 1995
6	Erik Nevland	Bury (H)	28 October 1998
7	Jesper Blomqvist	Everton (A)	31 October 1998
8	Jaap Stam	Leicester City (A)	16 January 1999
9	Sylvan Ebanks-Blake	Barnet (H)	26 October 2005
10	Chris Eagles	Everton (A)	28 April 2007

There are 82 United players who have scored just one goal for the club. Among them are Champions League winners (Blomqvist, Schmeichel and Stam) and Youth Cup winners (Cooke, Eagles, Ebanks-Blake, Kinsey), but none surely had as significant an impact as Harry Stafford. He played for the club between 1896 and 1903, making 200 appearances in all, and became captain in 1897. A stalwart defender who was committed to breaking up opposition attacks, he was born in Crewe and started his career at his hometown club. But Stafford wasn't content with merely being a player, he was a major fund-raiser for the club. When Newton Heath, as United was originally known, was on the verge of going bankrupt in April 1902, he helped find new investors. At a public meeting in New Islington Hall, Ancoats, he announced that local brewer John Henry Davies had agreed to put up the money that would save the club. Within a few years, United had won the league, the FA Cup and built Old Trafford, which is why he is a true one-goal wonder.

MOST GOALS IN THE CHAMPIONS LEAGUE*

	Player	CL Career	Appearances	Goals
1	Ruud van Nistelrooy	2001–06	47	38
2	Ryan Giggs	1993–	136	28
3	Paul Scholes	1994–2011	128	25
3	Wayne Rooney	2004–	63	25
5	Ole Gunnar Solskjaer	1996–2007	81	20
6	Andrew Cole	1996–2001	49	19
7	Cristiano Ronaldo	2003–09	55	16
8	David Beckham	1994–2003	81	15
9	Denis Law	1965–69	18	14
9	Roy Keane	1993–2005	80	14

When Ruud van Nistelrooy snapped his cruciate ligaments just before he was due to sign for United in 2000, Sir Alex Ferguson was happy to wait a year until he recovered before signing up the striker for a seemingly huge fee of £19 million from PSV Eindhoven. It proved to be well worth the wait and excellent business, as the Dutchman became one of the Reds' most lethal predators in the box, scoring goal after goal. Indeed, it was in the penalty area that he was at his most deadly, almost never scoring from further out. His strike rate was special whatever the level he was playing at, but to average four goals in every five Champions League matches was outstanding. His best campaign was 2002–03, when he scored 14 goals in 11 matches, failing to hit the target in just one of his appearances. In 2004–05, when Wayne Rooney burst on the scene with a debut hat-trick, van Nistelrooy soon topped it with four against Sparta Prague, the only United player to achieve this feat in the Champions League era.

*Includes the European Cup.

MOST APPEARANCES IN THE CHAMPIONS LEAGUE OVERALL

	Player	Teams	Appearances
1	Raul	Real Madrid, Schalke 04	144
2	Paolo Maldini	AC Milan	139
3	Ryan Giggs	Manchester United	136
4	Roberto Carlos	Real Madrid, Fenerbahce	128
4	Paul Scholes	Manchester United	128
6	Clarence Seedorf	Ajax, Real Madrid, AC Milan	122
7	Xavi	Barcelona	116
8	Gary Neville	Manchester United	115
8	Andriy Shevchenko	Dynamo Kyiv, AC Milan, Chelsea	115
10	Thierry Henry	Monaco, Juventus, Arsenal, Barcelona	114

The 2011 Champions League semi-finals paired the Spanish giants Real Madrid and Barcelona in one tie, and brought together three of the most experienced performers in Champions League history (Raul, Giggs and Scholes) as United took on Schalke in the other semi. By the end of the tie, each of them would hold a record. The Spaniard had left Real Madrid after the 2009–10 season, having made his debut for them way back in 1994. Before the first leg, Raul (who has scored the most goals in Champions League history with 71) spoke warmly of United, whom he had considered joining after Madrid, and in particular of the Welshman: 'I would love to swap shirts with Ryan Giggs after the game. It would be a great honour.' United won the away leg 2–0 thanks to goals from Giggs (who thus became the oldest scorer in the tournament's history) and Wayne Rooney. United won the second leg 4–1 to record the biggest aggregate win in a Champions League semi-final; Paul Scholes was booked to earn the record for most yellow cards in the tournament.

FWA FOOTBALLERS OF THE YEAR

	Player	Season
1	Johnny Carey	1948–49
2	Bobby Charlton	1965–66
3	George Best	1967–68
4	Eric Cantona	1995–96
5.	Roy Keane	1999–2000
6	Teddy Sheringham	2000–01
7	Cristiano Ronaldo	2006–07
8	Cristiano Ronaldo	2007–08
9	Wayne Rooney	2009–10

Johnny Carey became the second winner of the Football Writers' Association's top honour, a year after Stanley Matthews had received the inaugural award. The fact that Carey should be mentioned in such company gives an idea of how well respected United's post-war captain was. Carey had made his debut for United in September 1937, but the war deprived him of much of his career. By the time normal football resumed in 1946–47, he was 27 and had made fewer than 50 league appearances. He not only captained United to the FA Cup in 1948 but also to the league title in 1952. Uniquely, he captained both Northern Ireland and the Republic of Ireland. Renowned as a true gentleman of the game, Carey was a versatile footballer who could play either at full-back or half-back. During his 344 appearances for United he played in every position on the field, barring left-wing, even once lining up as the goal-keeper in February 1953. He retired after that season, going on to have a successful career as a manager.

UNITED'S FIRST TEN GOALSCORERS IN THE PREMIER LEAGUE

	Player	Opponent	Date	Score
1	Mark Hughes	Sheffield United	15 August 1992	1–2
2	Denis Irwin	Ipswich Town	22 August 1992	1–1
3	Dion Dublin	Southampton	24 August 1992	1–0
4	Ryan Giggs	Nottingham Forest	29 August 1992	2–0
5	Andrei Kanchelskis	Leeds United	6 September 1992	2–0
6	Steve Bruce	Leeds United	6 September 1992	2–0
7	Brian McClair	Everton	12 September 1992	2–0
8	Paul Ince	Manchester City	6 December 1992	2–1
9	Eric Cantona	Chelsea	19 December 1992	1–1
10	Lee Sharpe	Coventry City	28 December 1992	5–0

Mark Hughes had the honour of scoring United's first goal in the new Premier League, which began its inaugural season on 15 August 1992. The goal came in the second half in front of 28,070 fans at Bramall Lane. But United's campaign got off to the worst possible start, with a 2–1 defeat. Following the disappointment of the season before, when late slip-ups allowed Leeds United to take the title, it was a worrying sign. After a 3–0 home defeat to Everton, it was Denis Irwin who scored United's first Premier League goal at Old Trafford to secure a 1–1 draw against Ipswich – three games gone and United were 20th in the table. It was a poor start, but Hughes went on to have the most prolific season of his second spell with the Reds, scoring 15 league goals as United ended up taking their long-awaited first league title in 26 years by a massive ten-point margin from Aston Villa. United's only other Premier League goalscorers that first season were Paul Parker, Gary Pallister and Bryan Robson.

MOST APPEARANCES FOR UNITED
BY INTERNATIONAL PLAYERS

	Player	Career	Appearances
1	Peter Schmeichel	1991–99	398
2	Ole Gunnar Solskjaer	1996–2007	366
3	Mikael Silvestre	1999–2007	361
4	Cristiano Ronaldo	2003–09	292
5	Edwin van der Sar	2005–11	266
6	Patrice Evra	2006–	245
7	Nemanja Vidic	2006–	233
8	Ruud van Nistelrooy	2001–06	219
9	Eric Cantona	1992–97	185
10	Ji-Sung Park	2005–	177

When Ji-Sung Park joined United in the summer of 2005, signed from PSV Eindhoven for a fee of about £4 million, most Reds fans knew little about him. That isn't the case in his native South Korea, where he is the most famous footballer his country has ever produced, and he now has 100 caps for his national side. He grew up in Suwon outside Seoul, and recently opened a soccer training school there. His father also claimed that one of the keys to helping him develop physically was providing him with frog extract, a traditional medicine. Having made 44 appearances in his first campaign, he found himself rather edged out of things for the next two seasons. But his unstoppable workrate and capacity to play anywhere in midfield meant that he has become an increasingly vital cog in United's machine, almost always selected for the most vital matches. Now aged 30, he has helped United become even more popular in Eastern Asia, and receives more fanmail at Carrington than any other player.

MOST GOALS FOR UNITED BY INTERNATIONAL PLAYERS

	Player	Career	Goals
1	Ruud van Nistelrooy	2001–06	150
2	**Ole Gunnar Solskjaer**	**1996–2007**	**126**
3	Cristiano Ronaldo	2003–09	118
4	Eric Cantona	1992–97	82
5	Dwight Yorke	1998–2002	66
6	Dimitar Berbatov	2008–	47
7	Louis Saha	2004–08	42
8	Andrei Kanchelskis	1991–95	36
9	Carlos Tevez	2007–09	34
10	Nani	2007–	27

Norwegian striker Ole Gunnar Solskjaer is a true United legend, hugely popular with the fans, and one of the most lethal finishers in the modern era. He was largely unheralded when he joined United from Molde in the summer of 1996 for a fee of about £1.5 million, having made his international debut earlier in the season. It didn't take long for the Red Army to understand why Alex Ferguson had signed the 23-year-old, as he scored within a few minutes of coming off the bench to equalise against Blackburn Rovers. It was a story that would be repeated many times during his stay at Old Trafford, most famously, of course, in the 1999 Champions League final. His most prolific season came in 2001–02, when he scored 25 times. Although he was regularly targeted by other managers wanting to recruit such a proven goalscorer, he remained at United until injury finally forced him to retire. After doing so, he stayed with the Reds in a coaching capacity until former club Molde approached him to take charge in the 2010–11 season.

THE TEAMS UNITED HAVE NEVER FACED*

1	Cheltenham Town
2	Dagenham & Redbridge
3	Gillingham
4	Macclesfield Town
5	Morecambe
6	Shrewsbury Town
7	Stevenage
8	**Torquay United**
9	AFC Wimbledon
10	Wycombe Wanderers

Of the above teams, both Gillingham and Torquay were elected to the Football League in the 1920s and so are the sides that have avoided United for the longest. Torquay, of course, have one big connection with the Reds: they sold Lee Sharpe to United in 1988 for a fee of £180,000, rising to £300,000. Sharpe, who was raised in the West Midlands, was given a trial by Torquay at the end of the 1986–87 season and immediately impressed them, so was signed up on apprentice terms for the following campaign. Under manager Cyril Knowles, he played 14 times for Torquay, scoring three goals. His last game for them, against Scunthorpe United on 7 May 1988, attracted a crowd of 4,989; his league debut for United, against West Ham at Old Trafford, was played in front of 39,941. In total, he played 263 times for United, scoring 36 goals, including a famous hat-trick at Highbury against Arsenal in the League Cup, before eventually being sold to Leeds in August 1996 for £4.5 million.

*Among the 92 Football League teams in 2011–12.

THE CELTIC CONNECTION

	Player	United Debut	Appearances	Goals
1	Jimmy Delaney	31 August 1946	184	28
2	Tommy Bogan	8 October 1949	33	7
3	**Pat Crerand**	**23 February 1963**	397	15
4	Lou Macari	20 January 1973	401	97
5	Brian McClair	15 August 1987	471	127
6	Lee Martin	9 May 1988	109	2
7	Dion Dublin	15 August 1992	17	3
8	Roy Keane	7 August 1993	480	51
9	Liam Miller	11 August 2004	22	2
10	Henrik Larsson	7 January 2007	13	3

In addition to the above list of those who have played for both clubs, former Red Gordon Strachan also managed Celtic. But one of the most significant recruits to United from Celtic was undoubtedly Paddy Crerand, who came to Old Trafford for a fee of £53,000 in February 1963. Busby was in the process of rebuilding his side after Munich, having recruited Denis Law at the start of the season and David Herd the year before. Used as a creative wing-half, Crerand ensured the supply lines to the forwards and Bobby Charlton were working well, but he was also a fierce tackler who could break up the opposition play. By the end of his first campaign, he had an FA Cup winner's medal, and his vital influence on the team was clear to see. Within another two years, United were champions again. He played for United until the end of the 1970–71 season, before moving on to the coaching staff for a few years. Fiercely loyal to United, he now works on MUTV.

EARLIEST MATCHES PLAYED IN A SEASON

	Date	Year	Opposition	Result	Competition
1	1 August	1999	Arsenal	1–2	C Shield
2	3 August	1997	Chelsea	1–1	C Shield
3	5 August	2007	Chelsea	1–1	C Shield
4	7 August	1993	Arsenal	1–1	C Shield
5	8 August	1999	Everton	1–1	Prem Lg
5	8 August	2004	Arsenal	1–3	C Shield
5	**8 August**	**2010**	**Chelsea**	**3–1**	**C Shield**
8	9 August	1969	Crystal Palace	2–2	Div 1
8	9 August	1998	Arsenal	0–3	C Shield
8	9 August	2005	Debreceni	3–0	CL Qual
8	9 August	2009	Chelsea	2–2	C Shield

When United won the Community Shield at the start of the 2010–11 campaign, it was the earliest victory in the football calendar in the club's history. The traditional season opener gave Reds fans their first chance to see two debutants: Chris Smalling, who came on for Fabio, and Javier 'Chicharito' Hernandez, who replaced Ji-Sung Park. It was the latter who had the most immediate impact, as he scored United's second after Antonio Valencia had given his side the lead late in the first half. Hernandez had been signed for a fee of about £6 million from his hometown club Chivas de Guadalajara ahead of the World Cup, where he impressed for Mexico. Valencia set up the 22-year-old with a great cross from the right. Chicharito got his shot all wrong, and it looped up to hit him in the face – and rebounded into the net. It was the first of 20 goals he would score in his impressive debut season, as United's first Mexican player became an instant hit with the fans and his team-mates.

LATEST MATCHES PLAYED IN A SEASON

	Date	Year	Opposition	Result	Competition
1	16 June	1965	Ferencvaros	1–2	Fairs Cup SF R
2	6 June	1965	Ferencvaros	0–1	Fairs Cup SF
3	31 May	1965	Ferencvaros	3–2	Fairs Cup SF
4	29 May	1968	Benfica	4–1	EC Final
5	28 May	2011	Barcelona	1–3	CL Final
6	27 May	2009	Barcelona	0–2	CL Final
7	26 May	1947	Sheffield United	6–2	Div 1
7	26 May	1983	Brighton & Hove A	4–0	FA Cup Final
7	26 May	1999	Bayern Munich	2–1	CL Final
10	25 May	1963	Leicester City	3–1	FA Cup Final

Despite some critics' complaints that the football season ends later and later every year, the record latest finish to a campaign for United came way back in 1965, when the Inter-Cities' Fairs Cup did not end until an incredible seven weeks after the Reds had been crowned league champions. In those days, away goals did not count as double, and United had to return to the Nep Stadion in Budapest on 16 June for the decider after the tie ended 3–3 on aggregate, as they had lost home advantage on the toss of a coin. The winner would meet Juventus in the final a week later. In front of a passionate crowd of 75,000, United fell two goals behind, only for John Connelly, the right-wing who had been signed from Burnley at the start of the season, to pull back a goal. It wasn't enough, but at least United had the consolation they would be back in Europe the following campaign, which (astonishingly enough) started with the Charity Shield less than two months later.

FIRST LEAGUE TEAM FOR UNITED

	Player	Career	Appearances	Goals
1	Jimmy Warner	1892–93	22	0
2	John Clements	1891–94	42	0
3	Jim Brown	1892–93	7	0
4	George Perrins	1892–96	102	0
5	Willie Stewart	1890–95	87	5
6	**Fred Erentz**	**1892–1902**	**310**	**9**
7	Alf Farman	1889–95	61	28
8	Jimmy Coupar	1892–1902	34	10
9	Bob Donaldson	1892–97	155	66
10	Adam Carson	1892	13	3
11	William Mathieson	1892–94	10	2

In 1892 Newton Heath finally gained access to the Football League, four seasons after its creation, when the league was expanded to 16 teams. The Heathens' first game was at a rainy Ewood Park on 3 September 1892 against Blackburn Rovers in front of a crowd of about 8,000. Rovers were one of the top sides of the period, having won the FA Cup in 1890 and 1891, so it was a tough baptism and the home side went 3–0 up in 15 minutes. Bob Donaldson scored Newton Heath's first goal, and the final score was a respectable 4–3 defeat, with Jimmy Coupar and Alf Farman also scoring. But it was Fred Erentz, who was born near Dundee in 1870, who would go on to have the longest career with the club. In fact, he would play throughout the entire existence of Newton Heath as a Football League side, retiring with a knee injury in 1902, just as the club changed its name to Manchester United.

FIRST PREMIER LEAGUE TEAM FOR UNITED

	Player	Career	Appearances	Goals
1	Peter Schmeichel	1991–99	398	1
2	Denis Irwin	1990–2002	529	33
3	Clayton Blackmore	1984–93	245	26
4	Steve Bruce	1987–96	414	51
5	**Darren Ferguson**	**1991–93**	**30**	**0**
6	Gary Pallister	1989–98	437	15
7	Andrei Kanchelskis	1991–95	161	36
8	Paul Ince	1989–95	281	29
9	Brian McClair	1987–98	471	127
10	Mark Hughes	1983–95	467	163
11	Ryan Giggs	1991–	876	159

United started the new era of Premier League football at Sheffield United's Bramall Lane. Brian Deane struck for the hosts in the first half (the first goal in Premier League history), and after the interval United finished up beaten 2–1, despite a goal from Mark Hughes. Alex Ferguson's main summer signing, Dion Dublin, made his debut as a substitute. He had been brought in to give the Reds an additional aerial threat, partly because the Old Trafford pitch did not suit the slick passing game the manager wanted to play. Incredibly, eight of the starting XI would play 40 or more league games that campaign, with the manager's son being one of the few who didn't establish a regular place, though he did pick up a title medal at the end of the season. The following year he was transferred to Wolves, and later played for Wrexham for eight years before moving into management, taking Peterborough into the Championship in 2011–12, having managed Preston North End earlier in the campaign.

BIGGEST WINS IN THE FA CUP

	Opposition	Venue	Date	Round	Score
1	Yeovil Town	Maine Road	12 February 1949	5th	8–0
2	West Manchester	Bank Street	12 December 1896	3rd Q	7–0
2	Accrington Stanley	Bank Street	1 November 1902	3rd Q	7–0
4	Northampton Town	County Ground	7 February 1970	5th	8–2
5	Brentford	Old Trafford	14 January 1928	3rd	7–1
6	Bournemouth	Maine Road	8 January 1949	3rd	6–0
6	West Ham United	Old Trafford	26 January 2003	4th	6–0
8	Staple Hill	Bank Street	13 January 1906	1st	7–2
9	Blackburn Rovers	Bank Street	20 February 1909	3rd	6–1

The FA Cup often throws up some intriguing ties, as United found recently when they met non-League Burton Albion and Crawley Town. However, their game against Staple Hill from the Bristol area in the 1906 FA Cup certainly rates as one of the more unexpected pairings. That season, United finally won promotion to the First Division under the inspired management of Ernest Mangnall, as well as reaching the FA Cup quarter-finals for only the second time in their history. But their Cup run began with a game against the amateur Western League Division Two side. It was their first appearance in the FA Cup proper, and the experience was not a happy one – John Beddow scored a hat-trick for United, supported by two from Jack Picken and one each from Jack Allan and Harry Williams. To make matters worse for the visitors, before the game Liberal candidate for Manchester North West, Winston Churchill, practised his penalty kicks, doubtless before encouraging the 7,560 crowd to go and vote for him in the general election that day. Happily for him, he emerged with 56 per cent of the vote to beat his Conservative rival.

BIGGEST DEFEATS IN THE FA CUP

	Opposition	Venue	Date	Round	Score
1	Burnley	Turf Moor	13 February 1901	1st R	7–1
2	Sheffield Wednesday	Hillsborough	20 February 1904	2nd	6–0
3	Sheffield Wednesday	Old Trafford	1 February 1961	4th R	7–2
4	Preston North End	Deepdale	18 January 1890	1st	6–1
5	Arsenal	Highbury	30 January 1937	4th	5–0
6	Blackburn Rovers	Ewood Park	17 February 1894	2nd R	5–1
6	Derby County	Baseball Ground	19 February 1896	2nd R	5–1
6	West Bromwich Albion	Old Trafford	11 January 1939	3rd R	5–1
9	Blackburn Rovers	Ewood Park	21 January 1893	1st	4–0
9	Tottenham Hotspur	White Hart Lane	3 February 1923	2nd	4–0
9	Bristol Rovers	Eastville	7 January 1956	3rd	4–0

United have lost FA Cup ties on 97 occasions, as well as four other times when they have been beaten on penalty kicks. The above list shows the worst of those defeats, and surely the most surprising occasion came against Bristol Rovers in 1956. Rovers were a decent Second Division outfit at the time, but throughout their entire history they have never appeared in the top flight. United, by contrast, were on their way to becoming the runaway champions, eventually finishing 11 points clear of their nearest rivals. Almost all United's regular team played that day, with Duncan Edwards the only one who missed the game, his place taken by Jeff Whitefoot. Legendary journalist Desmond Hackett described the Rovers side in the *Daily Express* as the '£110 team with a million-dollar touch of class'. Alfie Biggs (2), Barrie Meyer and Geoff Bradford were Rovers' scorers. Meyer went on to win greater fame as a Test match umpire, standing in the cricket World Cup finals of 1979 and 1983.

EDWIN VAN DER SAR'S CLEAN SHEETS

	Opposition	Venue	Date	Score
1	Stoke City	Home	15 November	5–0
2	Aston Villa	Away	22 November	0–0
3	Manchester City	Away	30 November	1–0
4	Sunderland	Home	6 December	1–0
5	Tottenham Hotspur	Away	13 December	0–0
6	Stoke City	Away	26 December	1–0
7	Middlesbrough	Home	29 December	1–0
8	Chelsea	Home	11 January	3–0
9	Wigan Athletic	Home	14 January	1–0
10	Bolton Wanderers	Away	17 January	1–0
11	West Bromwich Albion	Away	27 January	5–0
12	Everton	Home	31 January	1–0
13	West Ham United	Away	8 February	1–0
14	Fulham	Home	18 February	3–0

In 2008–09, Edwin van der Sar set a Premier League record of 1,311 minutes without conceding a goal. After Samir Nasri scored for Arsenal after 48 minutes on 8 November, United's Dutch keeper kept 14 successive clean sheets. He missed the game on 21 February against Blackburn (when United won 2–1), but was back on 4 March for the trip to St James' Park when Peter Lovenkrands hit the target after nine minutes. That fabulous defensive effort sped United to the top of the table, and once they got there they were never overhauled. Van der Sar had been signed from Fulham in summer 2005, and retired aged 40 after the 2011 Champions League final.

PENALTY SHOOT-OUTS

	Opposition	Date	Competition	Score	Shoot-Out
1	Videoton	20 Mar 1985	UEFA Cup QF	1–1	4–5
2	Southampton	5 Feb 1992	FA Cup 4th R	2–2	2–4
3	Arsenal	7 Aug 1993	Charity Shield	1–1	5–4
4	Torpedo Moscow	29 Sep 1993	UEFA Cup 1st	0–0	3–4
5	Chelsea	3 Aug 1997	Charity Shield	1–1	4–2
6	Arsenal	10 Aug 2003	Community Shield	1–1	4–3
7	Arsenal	21 May 2005	FA Cup Final	0–0	4–5
8	Chelsea	5 Aug 2007	Community Shield	1–1	3–0
9	Chelsea	21 May 2008	Champions League F	1–1	6–5
10	Portsmouth	10 Aug 2008	Community Shield	0–0	3–1
11	Tottenham Hotspur	1 Mar 2009	League Cup Final	0–0	4–1
12	Everton	19 Apr 2009	FA Cup Semi-final	0–0	2–4
13	Chelsea	9 Aug 2009	Community Shield	2–2	1–4

United made history in 1992 when they became the first top-flight side to be knocked out of the FA Cup in a penalty shoot-out. Prior to that season, an unlimited number of FA Cup replays was allowed, but from 1991–92 it was restricted to one replay. United had drawn the tie 0–0 at The Dell, and returned to Old Trafford for the replay against relegation-threatened Saints. Southampton failed to read the script, and went into a 2–1 half-time lead, Andrei Kanchelskis scoring for United. In the second half, Brian McClair equalised, but there were no more goals, even after 30 minutes of extra time. Trailing 4–2 in the shoot-out, it was left to 18-year-old Ryan Giggs to keep United in the hunt, but his penalty was saved by Tim Flowers and United were out.

BEST LEAGUE SEASONS AT HOME*

	Season	Played	Won	Drawn	Lost	Goal Diff	Ave Points
1	2010–11	19	18	1	0	37	2.89
2	1904–05	17	16	0	1	50	2.82
3	2007–08	19	17	1	1	40	2.74
4	1955–56	21	18	3	0	31	2.714
5	1899–1900	17	15	1	1	33	2.706
6	2002–03	19	16	2	1	30	2.63
6	2008–09	19	16	2	1	30	2.63
8	1966–67	21	17	4	0	38	2.62
9	1903–04	17	14	2	1	28	2.59
10	1995–96	19	15	4	0	27	2.58
10	1999–2000	19	15	4	0	33	2.58
10	2009–10	19	16	1	2	40	2.58

United have traditionally been very successful at home, thanks in part to the passionate support of their fans, who always ensure any visitors will have a difficult time. Perhaps surprisingly, three of the club's best seasons at home came at their dilapidated ground at Bank Street. However, a new record was set in 2010–11 when United not only went undefeated, but dropped just two points at home all campaign. West Bromwich Albion were the team who prevented United from having a 100 per cent record, managing a 2–2 draw. Javier Hernandez scored his first goal at the ground and then Nani put the Reds 2–0 up before half time. After the interval, Patrice Evra gave away an own goal before Edwin van der Sar made an uncharacteristic error, dropping the ball to allow the equaliser. After that there were no slip-ups, as United won 15 consecutive home games to secure the title.

*Assuming three points for a win.

BEST LEAGUE SEASONS AWAY FROM HOME★

	Season	Played	Won	Drawn	Lost	Goal Diff	Ave Points
1	1905–06	19	13	3	3	20	2.21
1	1999–2000	19	13	3	3	9	2.21
1	2001–02	19	13	3	3	19	2.21
1	**2006–07**	**19**	**13**	**3**	**3**	**22**	**2.21**
5	1956–57	21	14	4	3	19	2.19
6	2008–09	19	12	4	3	14	2.11
7	1993–94	21	13	5	3	16	2.10
8	2005–06	19	12	3	4	9	2.05
9	2009–10	19	11	3	5	18	1.89
10	2003–04	19	11	2	6	7	1.84
10	2004–05	19	10	5	4	13	1.84
10	2007–08	19	10	5	4	18	1.84

What is most noticeable about this list is how many of United's best away seasons have come during the Premier League era. By virtue of better goal difference, the 2006–07 campaign proved to be the Reds' most fruitful of all on their travels. The only defeats came at West Ham United (1–0 in December), Arsenal (2–1 in January) and Portsmouth (2–1 in April). United's away resolve was never more tested than against Everton, in late April, when they fell 2–0 behind and it wasn't until after the hour mark that John O'Shea pulled back a goal. Minutes later, United old boy Phil Neville miskicked into his own net for the equaliser, before Wayne Rooney gave United the lead against *his* former club and Chris Eagles added a fourth at the end. 'The champion feeling is there,' commented Sir Alex. After a win at Manchester City in the next away game, he was right.

★Assuming three points for a win.

TEN SURPRISING PLAYERS FOR UNITED

		Debut	*Apps*	*Other Career*
1	Peter Beardsley	6 October 1982	1	England international
2	Alan Brazil	25 August 1984	41	Broadcaster
3	Frank Buckley	29 September 1906	3	Manager
4	Garth Crooks	19 November 1983	7	Broadcaster
5	Andy Goram	14 April 2001	2	Scotland international
6	Harold Hardman	19 September 1908	4	United chairman
7	Harry McShane	13 September 1950	57	Father of actor Ian
8	Les Olive	11 April 1953	2	United club secretary
9	Arnold Sidebottom	23 April 1973	20	England cricketer
10	Walter Winterbottom	28 November 1936	27	England manager

Few men can have had quite as long and varied an involvement with United as Harold Hardman. In the years before the First World War, the England international made his debut as an inside-forward in the Manchester derby, helping United to a 2–1 victory at City's Hyde Road ground. He made three more appearances, at left-wing, during the 1908–09 season – United's last full campaign at Bank Street before they moved to Old Trafford. He subsequently became a lawyer, and joined the board in the 1920s. When James Gibson saved the club from bankruptcy in 1930, he was one of those removed by the new man, but his experience was vital and he was soon brought back. After the Second World War, he was the heir apparent to the now-frail Gibson, eventually succeeding him. He was still club chairman at the time of the Munich Air Disaster – one reason he wasn't on the trip is that on a previous flight the heating had been accidentally switched off by one of the players, and he had caught hypothermia.

EIGHT DEGREES OF SEPARATION

	Player	Debut	Last time together	Last game
1	Ryan Giggs	2 March 1991	16 April 1994	–
2	Bryan Robson	7 October 1981	6 January 1982	8 May 1994
3	Sammy McIlroy	6 November 1971	11 November 1972	6 January 1982
4	Bobby Charlton	6 October 1956	26 October 1957	28 April 1973
5	Ray Wood	3 December 1949	21 February 1953	4 October 1958
6	Johnny Carey	25 September 1937	10 April 1939	25 April 1953
7	Tom Manley	5 December 1931	4 February 1933	10 April 1939
8	Joe Spence	30 August 1919	7 May 1921	1 April 1933
9	Billy Meredith	1 January 1907	–	7 May 1921

To get back from a winner of United's 19th title in 2010–11 to a winner of the Reds' first title in 1907–08 (both, coincidentally, Welsh wingers), takes just eight steps between players who lined up alongside each other. The only one of the above list in the post-war era to miss out on lifting the league trophy is Sammy McIlroy, but in every other sense he was a huge part of United's history. Famously known as 'the last Busby Babe', McIlroy was the final recruit of the legendary manager, joining the club as a 15-year-old apprentice in 1969. On his debut, against Manchester City two years later, he scored in a 3–3 draw, drawing inevitable comparisons with his fellow Ulsterman in the side, George Best. When he was eventually sold to Stoke City for £350,000 by Ron Atkinson early in 1982, he was playing under his sixth United manager. He picked up only one major honour: the FA Cup in 1977. A skilful mid-fielder, he had good pace and an eye for goal, scoring 71 times in 419 appearances (for comparison, Bryan Robson scored 99 goals in 461 games).

MOST RECENT WORLD CUP GOALS SCORED
BY CURRENT UNITED PLAYERS

	Player	Team	Opposition	Date
1	Javier Hernandez	Mexico	Argentina	27 June 2010
2	Javier Hernandez	Mexico	France	17 June 2010
3	Ji-Sung Park	South Korea	Greece	12 June 2010
4	Ji-Sung Park	South Korea	France	18 June 2006
5	Cristiano Ronaldo	Portugal	Iran	17 June 2006
6	Ruud van Nistelrooy	Netherlands	Ivory Coast	16 June 2006
7	Diego Forlan	Uruguay	Senegal	11 June 2002
8	David Beckham	England	Argentina	7 June 2002
9	Quinton Fortune	South Africa	Paraguay	2 June 2002
10	David Beckham	England	Colombia	26 June 1998
11	Paul Scholes	England	Tunisia	15 June 1998

Only two United players have scored for England in the last seven
World Cup finals, but the goal from Paul Scholes in England's
opening fixture in France 98 was something pretty special.
Receiving the ball on the edge of the penalty area two minutes
before the end, he somehow kept on his feet after evading a scyth-
ing tackle. He was, however, forced away from goal, but this
enabled him to shoot on the turn and curl it with his right foot into
the top right-hand corner of the goal, past Choukri El Ouaer. It
gave England a 2–0 victory in the Stade Velodrome, Marseille.
Scholes had made his debut for England just over a year before,
against South Africa at Old Trafford on 24 May 1997, when he was
one of four United players to appear – along with David Beckham,
Nicky Butt and Phil Neville. He retired from international duty in
2004 with 66 caps and 14 goals.

THE FRENCH FOREIGN LEGION

	Player	Debut	Appearances	Goals
1	Eric Cantona	6 December 1992	185	82
2	William Prunier	30 December 1995	2	0
3	Mikael Silvestre	11 September 1999	361	10
4	Fabien Barthez	13 August 2000	139	0
5	Laurent Blanc	8 September 2001	75	4
6	David Bellion	27 August 2003	40	8
7	Louis Saha	31 January 2004	124	42
8	Patrice Evra	14 January 2006	245	3
9	Gabriel Obertan	27 October 2009	28	1
10	Paul Pogba	Awaiting debut	0	0

When *l'enfant terrible* of French football joined Manchester United, few could have known what was in store. Beforehand, Eric Cantona had played for five different clubs in France and spent less than a year at Leeds – and he was only 26. No one doubted his talent, but he had a catalogue of disputes behind him, notoriously once calling the national team manager a 'shitbag'. But Alex Ferguson had seen how he had inspired the Leeds side in the title run-in in 1991–92, so when they offered him for just £1 million he didn't hesitate – it remains one of his greatest transfer coups. Cantona transformed the club: his confidence – some called it arrogance – spread through the side; his goals and creative play gave United a real cutting edge; the fans loved him, and he loved them back; and, perhaps above all, he brought a new professionalism and dedication to training that rubbed off on the young players coming through at that time, among them Giggs, Beckham and Scholes. With Cantona, United dominated the early Premier League era.

MOST APPEARANCES FOR UNITED
BY WELSH PLAYERS

	Player	Career	Appearances
1	Ryan Giggs	1991–	876
2	Mark Hughes	1983–95	467
3	Billy Meredith	1907–21	335
4	Ray Bennion	1921–32	301
5	Clayton Blackmore	1984–93	245
6	Tom Jones	1924–37	200
7	Harry Thomas	1922–30	135
8	Jack Warner	1938–50	116
9	Mickey Thomas	1978–81	110
10	Tommy Bamford	1934–38	109

Neath-born Clayton Blackmore was always a popular figure in the
United squad and among the fans. Never one of the big stars, he
could turn out in a very wide range of positions. He came up
through the youth ranks and made his debut for the Reds in the
final game of the 1983–84 season, aged 19, but it took him a few
seasons to become a regular starter. In 1990–91, he had his most
hectic campaign, missing just three fixtures and starting all the
rest (57 in total), helping United to European Cup-Winners' Cup
success. In the final, he made a vital clearance to prevent a late
Barcelona equaliser. In the quarter-finals, he scored a spectacular
goal from a long-range free kick against Montpellier. He also scored
the goal in the Charity Shield at the start of the season that enabled
the Reds to share the trophy with Liverpool. He left United in
1994 to join Bryan Robson at Middlesbrough, but in 2010
returned to the club as a coach of the Under-15 Academy team.

MOST GOALS FOR UNITED
BY WELSH PLAYERS

	Player	Career	Goals
1	Mark Hughes	1983–95	163
2	Ryan Giggs	1991–	159
3	Tommy Bamford	1934–38	57
4	Billy Meredith	1907–21	36
5	Colin Webster	1953–58	31
6	Clayton Blackmore	1984–93	26
7	Mickey Thomas	1978–81	15
8	Bill Jackson	1899–1901	14
9	Harry Thomas	1922–30	13

While the top two names in this list are familiar to all United fans, Tommy Bamford will be unknown to most. He is, however, a legend in Wrexham, where a local brewer has been selling Tommy's Cask Lager to help raise funds for the club. Born in Port Talbot in 1905, Bamford scored a Wrexham club record 44 goals in Division Three (North) in the 1933–34 season and remains their all-time leading scorer. As United had almost joined them in that division after their worst-ever campaign, manager Scott Duncan knew he needed some extra firepower up front and snapped up the Welsh international. In partnership with fellow new signing George Mutch, United began the road to recovery, gaining promotion in 1936. While Bamford thrived at the higher level, top-scoring with 14 goals in 29 league appearances, many others struggled, and United came straight back down. As United's leading scorer again in 1937–38, he led the Reds to promotion, before leaving for Swansea Town. He won five caps for Wales between 1930 (when he scored against Scotland on his debut) and 1933.

MOST APPEARANCES AS A
SUBSTITUTE IN A SEASON

	Player	Season	Appearances
1	Diego Forlan	2002–03	30
2	David McCreery	1976–77	24
3	Teddy Sheringham	1999–2000	22
3	Ole Gunnar Solskjaer	1999–2000	22
3	John O'Shea	2006–07	22
6	Ole Gunnar Solskjaer	2000–01	21
6	John O'Shea	2007–08	21
8	Ole Gunnar Solskjaer	1998–99	20
8	Brian McClair	1996–97	20
8	Michael Owen	2009–10	20

The 2002–03 campaign was one of United's longest, with 63 fixtures in all, as the club won its eighth Premier League title. But for Diego Forlan it was a season he spent almost half of coming off the bench. The Uruguayan had joined the Reds in January 2002, but despite his all-action style the normally prolific striker signed from Argentine club Independiente for almost £7 million had failed to score in his first campaign. He finally broke his duck when he came off the bench, late on against Maccabi Haifa in the Champions League in September 2002; he was in the middle of a run of 11 successive substitute appearances. While the floodgates never quite opened for him at United, he will always be remembered for his brace at Anfield to secure a win over Liverpool. His shirt-twirling goal celebrations would now, of course, be punished. After leaving Old Trafford to make way for Wayne Rooney, he moved to Villarreal and then Atletico Madrid where he averaged better than a goal every two games, taking the latter to Europa League success in 2010.

EA SPORTS INDEX RESULTS FOR 2010–11

	Player	Ranking	Overall Position
1	Dimitar Berbatov	583	2nd
2	Nemanja Vidic	551	4th
3	Wayne Rooney	499	13th
4	Patrice Evra	474	18th
5	Nani	471	19th
6	Edwin van der Sar	429	31st
7	Darren Fletcher	390	59th
8	Javier Hernandez	349	92nd

The EA Sports Index is the official player rating index of the Barclays Premier League and is based on a combination of factors, including: time spent playing for a winning side, personal impact on a game (shots, tackles, etc.), total time spent playing, goals scored, assists and clean sheets. Eight United players made it into the Top 100 in 2010–11, the same number as in the previous season, with some others missing out due to lack of time on the pitch. As the joint leading scorer in the Premier League, Berbatov was officially the top-ranked forward, while Nemanja Vidic was the top-ranked defender, ahead of Vincent Kompany, Leighton Baines and John Terry. The new captain not only stopped the goals going in at one end, he also scored five at the other end. Arguably, none was more crucial than his headed equaliser five minutes from time on 13 November at Aston Villa, though his volley against the same side at Old Trafford was pretty special. Although his partnership with Rio Ferdinand has been the bedrock of United's defence for years, he also helped Chris Smalling through his first Old Trafford campaign, and in 2011–12 will have new recruit Phil Jones alongside him.

LONGEST CURRENT RUN OF SEASONS
IN THE TOP DIVISION

	Team	Joined Top Division	Period at Lower Level	Total*
1	Arsenal	1919–20	2 seasons	85
2	Everton	1954–55	3 seasons	57
3	Liverpool	1962–63	8 seasons	49
4	**Manchester United**	**1975–76**	**1 season**	**36**
5	Tottenham Hotspur	1978–79	1 season	33
6	Aston Villa	1988–89	1 season	23
7	Chelsea	1989–90	1 season	22
8	Blackburn Rovers	2001–02	2 seasons	10
8	Bolton Wanderers	2001–02	3 seasons	10
8	Fulham	2001–02	33 seasons	10

Only three teams have had a longer current unbroken run in the top division than Manchester United. The Reds' last spell out of the limelight came during 1974–75. In the years following Sir Matt Busby's retirement, the club had found it difficult to replace him and some of the players who had won so much during the 1960s. Eventually, under Tommy Docherty, they were relegated in 1974. But he used the period to help build an exciting new squad, while taking on a lower level of opposition helped the team regain some lost confidence. United had just one defeat in their first 16 games in the Second Division, with new centre-forward Stuart Pearson leading the way up front, aided by the creativity of Sammy McIlroy, Lou Macari, Willie Morgan and Gerry Daly. Further back, Brian Greenhoff, Martin Buchan, Alex Forsyth, Stewart Houston and Alex Stepney kept the defence tight. Finishing ten points clear of fourth place, promotion was always a certainty, but United also won the league, ending up three points clear of Aston Villa.

*To end of 2010–11 season.

LONGEST-SERVING MANAGERS IN
THE PREMIER LEAGUE

	Manager	Club	Appointed
1	Sir Alex Ferguson	Manchester United	November 1986
2	Arsene Wenger	Arsenal	September 1996
3	David Moyes	Everton	March 2002
4	Tony Pulis	Stoke City	June 2006
5	Mick McCarthy	Wolverhampton W	July 2006
6	Harry Redknapp	Tottenham Hotspur	October 2008
7	Steve Bruce	Sunderland	June 2009
8	Roberto Martinez	Wigan Athletic	June 2009
9	Paul Lambert	Norwich City	August 2009
10	Roberto Mancini	Manchester City	December 2009

If ever a list could show what sets Sir Alex Ferguson apart from other managers, this is it. By the end of the 2010–11 season, only two other Premier League managers had been at their clubs for five years or more: Arsene Wenger and David Moyes. Yet Sir Alex is in his 25th year at United. When he joined the club from Aberdeen, United had already gone 19 seasons without winning a league title. Turning things around and fulfilling United's obvious potential wasn't a simple task. What made Ferguson unique was that he decided he was going to revamp the club from top to bottom. United could always buy top players and challenge for honours that way, but he realised that wasn't enough: excellence had to be built into the club at all levels. Most other managers have to concentrate on getting the first team as high up the table as possible or face the sack. The board understood what he was doing and gave him the time to do it. United fans are still enjoying the results to this day.

MOST LEAGUE GAMES UNDEFEATED

	First Game	Lost to	Date Run Ended	Games
1	26 December 1998	Chelsea	3 October 1999	29
1	11 April 2010	Wolverhampton W	5 February 2011	29
3	4 February 1956	Everton	20 October 1956	26
4	19 September 1993	Chelsea	5 March 1994	22
5	20 February 2000	Arsenal	1 October 2000	21
5	28 December 2002	Southampton	31 August 2003	21
7	18 January 1936	Huddersfield Town	2 September 1936	20
7	27 December 1966	Everton	19 August 1967	20
7	7 November 2004	Norwich City	9 April 2005	20
10	24 September 1904	Lincoln City	11 February 1905	18

United set a new club record for league games undefeated that began midway through the 1998–99 campaign with a 3–0 win over Nottingham Forest on Boxing Day, thanks to two goals from the surprising source of Ronny Johnsen and another from Ryan Giggs. But it wasn't until the end of January that the Reds overhauled Chelsea to take top spot. Indeed, United went undefeated for the rest of the campaign in all competitions, famously going on to take the Treble of Premier League, FA Cup and Champions League. The next season, Sir Alex's team continued to set the pace and were top of the table at the end of September before heading to Stamford Bridge. Although Nicky Butt was sent off midway through the first half, United were already 2–0 down by then and ended up being trounced 5–0 – a disastrous end to their astonishing run of 20 wins and nine draws. It didn't prove to be a long-term setback, as the Reds went on to retain their Premier League title by the massive margin of 18 points.

MOST APPEARANCES FOR TOMMY DOCHERTY'S SIGNINGS

	Player	Career	Appearances	Goals
1	Lou Macari	1973–84	401	97
2	Steve Coppell	1975–83	396	70
3	Stewart Houston	1974–80	250	16
4	Stuart Pearson	1974–79	180	66
5	Gerry Daly	1973–77	142	32
6	Gordon Hill	1975–78	134	51
7	Jimmy Greenhoff	1976–80	123	36
8	Alex Forsyth	1973–77	119	5
9	Ashley Grimes	1977–83	107	11
10	Jim Holton	1973–74	69	5

Steve Coppell arguably proved to be Docherty's most significant signing. According to one story, he was recommended to the Doc by Bill Shankly, who approached United when Liverpool decided not to follow up on the tip; according to another, it was Busby's former No. 2, Jimmy Murphy, who brought him to United's attention; another account says it was scout Norman Scholes. No wonder many people wanted to claim the credit. At just £60,000 from Tranmere, he was a brilliant signing. With almost his first touch for United, wearing boots borrowed from Stuart Pearson, he set up the latter to score. Played out on the wide right, he was capable of being a flying winger; or else, under Dave Sexton, he could play in a more withdrawn role. He was adaptable, hard-working and reliable (setting a record for the most consecutive games played for United). For both England and United, he was always one of the first names on the teamsheet, until a knee injury playing for England against Hungary when aged just 28 brought his career to an end.

MOST APPEARANCES IN THE LEAGUE CUP

	Player	Career	Appearances
1	Bryan Robson	1981–94	51
2	Brian McClair	1987–98	45
3	Arthur Albiston	1974–88	40
4	Mark Hughes	1983–95	38
5	Ryan Giggs	1991–	37
6	**Gary Pallister**	**1989–98**	**36**
7	Alex Stepney	1966–78	35
8	**Steve Bruce**	**1987–96**	**34**
8	Mike Duxbury	1980–90	34
10	Denis Irwin	1990–2002	31

Gary Pallister and Steve Bruce formed one of the great centre-back partnerships in the history of Manchester United. It was appropriate that both men should be in action together when the club finally won its first League Cup, in 1992, beating Nottingham Forest 1–0, to make up for the disappointment when they had been losing finalists the previous campaign. As so often, it was the clean sheet they helped deliver at the back that proved just as decisive as the action up front. Pallister had joined the club from Middlesbrough for a British transfer record of £2.4 million in the summer of 1989, while Bruce had arrived from Norwich City on 19 December 1987 for £825,000. Both became stalwarts, even though Bruce gave away a penalty and broke his nose on his debut, while Pallister also took a little time to settle in at Old Trafford. However, in the two seasons that followed their League Cup success, the pair missed just three games between them, so consistent were their form and fitness. Bruce eventually succeeded Bryan Robson as captain of the side.

MOST GOALS IN THE LEAGUE CUP

	Player	Career	Appearances	Goals
1	Brian McClair	1987–98	45	19
2	Mark Hughes	1983–95	38	16
3	Lou Macari	1973–84	27	10
4	George Best	1963–74	25	9
4	Steve Coppell	1975–83	25	9
4	Norman Whiteside	1982–89	29	9
4	Lee Sharpe	1988–96	23	9
4	Ryan Giggs	1991–	37	9
4	Paul Scholes	1994–2011	21	9
10	Brian Kidd	1967–74	20	7
10	Bobby Charlton	1956–73	24	7
10	Louis Saha	2004–08	9	7
10	Ole Gunnar Solskjaer	1996–2007	11	7

Given United's excellent recent record in the League Cup, it is perhaps surprising that there aren't more current players on this list. But Sir Alex often likes to take the opportunity to rotate his squad when picking his sides for this competition. Because of this, Brian McClair's record looks certain to survive for many years to come. He scored his first League Cup goal on his debut in the tournament, against Hull City in September 1987 in a 5–0 win. But his most crucial goal came in the 1992 final, against Nottingham Forest. His strike, in the 14th minute, was enough to separate the two sides, and ensured that the Reds won a trophy for the third consecutive season. Lou Macari holds the record for scoring the most goals in a single campaign – seven in 1974–75, when United reached the semi-finals before being knocked out by Norwich City.

THE SAME XI – TWICE!

Squad No.	v Wigan	v Chelsea
1	Edwin van der Sar	Edwin van der Sar
22	John O'Shea	John O'Shea
15	Nemanja Vidic	Nemanja Vidic
12	Chris Smalling	Chris Smalling
3	Patrice Evra	Patrice Evra
24	Darren Fletcher	Darren Fletcher
16	Michael Carrick	Michael Carrick
18	Paul Scholes	Paul Scholes
17	**Nani**	**Nani**
10	Wayne Rooney	Wayne Rooney
14	Javier Hernandez	Javier Hernandez

On Tuesday 1 March 2011, Sir Alex Ferguson sent out the same team to play Chelsea at Stamford Bridge as he had in the Reds' previous game, at the DW Stadium against Wigan Athletic also in the Premier League, just three days earlier. Astonishingly, this was the first time in 165 games that he had done this. Sadly, having won 4–0 at Wigan, United then lost 2–1 to Chelsea. The previous occasion when he had picked the same side twice was late in the 2007–08 season, and five of the above line-up had appeared in that double, too: van der Sar, Evra, Carrick, Scholes and Nani. The Portuguese winger had joined United in the summer of 2007, aged 20. Nani had his best season yet in 2010–11, and was voted the Players' Player of the Year by the United squad. He was the leading provider of assists (with 18), and also had his most prolific campaign to date, scoring ten goals.

BIGGEST WINS AGAINST CHELSEA

	Date	Venue	Score	Scorers
1	26 December 1960	Old Trafford	6–0	Dawson 3, Nicholson 2, Charlton
2	17 April 1948	Maine Road	5–0	Pearson 2, Delaney, Mitten, Rowley
3	24 September 1938	Old Trafford	5–1	Carey, Manley, Redwood, Rowley, Smith
4	29 November 1947	Stamford Bridge	4–0	Morris 3, Rowley
4	13 March 1965	Old Trafford	4–0	Herd 2, Best, Law
4	14 May 1994	Wembley	4–0	Cantona 2, Hughes, McClair
7	2 September 1959	Stamford Bridge	6–3	Bradley 2, Viollet 2, Charlton, Quixall
8	23 August 1958	Old Trafford	5–2	Charlton 3, Dawson 2

Recently, United's biggest rivals for the title have undoubtedly been Chelsea. But it wasn't always that way. Indeed, you have to go back more than 50 years to find United's biggest win over the Londoners, and the star of the show that day was hat-trick hero Alex Dawson, a somewhat overlooked figure in the club's history. The forward was born in Aberdeen in February 1940 – just like Denis Law. Dawson joined United at 16 and made his debut the following year, scoring in each of his first three games for the club at the end of 1956–57. He was thrust into the limelight after Munich, having the daunting task of replacing Tommy Taylor. He scored in the first match after the disaster, then scored again (and had his nose broken) in the following game. In the 1958 FA Cup semi-final, he scored a hat-trick, the last man to do so, and became the youngest United player ever to hit three goals. But the pressure to live up to the legacy of the Babes was a heavy one, and despite having his most prolific season in 1960–61, scoring 20 goals, he was sold to Preston in October 1961 to make way for David Herd.

MOST RECENT HOME-GROWN ENGLAND PLAYERS

	Player	England debut	Caps	Goals
1	Danny Welbeck	29 March 2011	1	0
2	Kieran Richardson	28 May 2005	8	2
3	**Wes Brown**	**28 April 1999**	23	1
4	Paul Scholes	24 May 1997	66	14
5	Nicky Butt	29 March 1997	39	0
6	David Beckham	1 September 1996	115	17
7	Phil Neville	23 May 1996	59	0
8	Gary Neville	3 June 1995	85	0
9	Gary Bailey	26 March 1985	2	0
10	Mike Duxbury	16 November 1983	10	0

The 1990s were a golden period for United's home-grown talent when many of them not only rose through the club's ranks, but also went on to win international honours. Wes Brown was the last of that group. The Longsight-born defender became a part of the United set-up as early as 12, and made his senior debut at the age of 18 near the end of the 1997–98 season, when he won the Jimmy Murphy Young Player of the Year Award for the first time. Once described by Sir Alex as 'the best natural defender' in the club, Brown went on to make 362 appearances for the Reds, either in the heart of the defence or at right-back, which was where he played for much of the 2007–08 Champions League and Premier League-winning side. Injuries have often interrupted his career, and there is no doubt that had he stayed fit he would also have added to his 23 England caps, the most recent of which came in March 2010, almost 11 years after his debut. He was sold to Sunderland in July 2011.

TOMMY DOCHERTY'S TARTAN ARMY

	Player	Debut	Appearances	Goals
1	Alex Forsyth	6 January 1973	119	5
1	George Graham	6 January 1973	46	2
3	Jim Holton	20 January 1973	69	5
3	**Lou Macari**	**20 January 1973**	**401**	**97**
5	George Buchan	15 September 1973	4	0
6	Stewart Houston	1 January 1974	250	16
7	Jim McCalliog	16 March 1974	38	7
8	Arthur Albiston	9 October 1974	485	7
9	Steve Paterson	29 September 1976	10	0

When Tommy Docherty was appointed United manager at the end of 1972, the club already had Scots Martin Buchan, Ian Donald, John Fitzpatrick, Denis Law, Ted MacDougall, Willie Morgan and Willie Watson on its books. Obviously worried that this wasn't enough for a good Burns Night party, within a month Docherty had added four more to the list, the most significant of whom was Lou Macari; five more Scots would make their debuts later. The Celtic man, who played up front alongside Kenny Dalglish for the Glasgow club, was wanted by both United and Liverpool. Having chosen to come to Old Trafford for a then record-equalling fee of £200,000, he further endeared himself to the Stretford End by scoring on his debut against West Ham to save a point. Soon, he moved back into midfield, where he discovered his true role, finding the back of the net regularly (he scored 58 goals in four seasons from 1974–75 to 1977–78). After leaving United, he went into management between 1984 and 2002, and now works for MUTV as well as owning the chip shop at the end of Sir Matt Busby Way.

FIRST DIVISION TITLES

	Season	P	W	D	L	F	A	Pts
1	1907–08	38	23	6	9	81	48	52
2	1910–11	38	22	8	8	72	40	52
3	1951–52	42	23	11	8	95	52	57
4	1955–56	42	25	10	7	83	51	60
5	1956–57	42	28	8	6	103	54	64
6	1964–65	42	26	9	7	89	39	61
7	1966–67	42	24	12	6	84	45	60

In the years before the start of the Premier League in 1992–93, United won seven league titles. Most of United's titles came in pairs: the Ernest Mangnall side before the First World War; the Busby Babes in the mid 1950s and the Best/Law/Charlton team of the mid 1960s. The one exception to that was United's title-winning side of 1951–52. In the post-war era, Matt Busby had built up a team of experienced players who had gone through much – they were often quite literally battle-hardened. They played a brand of exciting, passing football and they had been runners-up in four of the first five post-war seasons. For many of that side, it was their last chance to win the league: John Aston, captain Johnny Carey, Allenby Chilton, Henry Cockburn, Jack Crompton, Stan Pearson and Jack Rowley had all been with the Reds since the end of the war. But there were some good, young players being groomed for the top, and the old brigade knew it was now or never. United's main rivals were Tottenham and Arsenal, and it was the latter who came to Old Trafford on the last day of the season, needing to beat United by seven goals to pinch the crown. There were seven goals, but six of them were for United, including a hat-trick for Rowley.

MOST RECENT JIMMY MURPHY YOUNG PLAYERS OF THE YEAR

	Player	Season	Apps (Goals)	Current Team
1	Ryan Tunnicliffe	2010–11	0	Manchester United
2	Will Keane	2009–10	0	Manchester United
3	**Federico Macheda**	**2008–09**	**27 (4)**	**Manchester United**
4	Danny Welbeck	2007–08	24 (5)	Manchester United
5	Craig Cathcart	2006–07	0	Blackpool
6	Darron Gibson	2005–06	58 (10)	Manchester United
7	Giuseppe Rossi	2004–05	14 (4)	Villarreal
8	Jonathan Spector	2003–04	7	West Ham United
9	Ben Collett	2002–03	0	Retired
10	Paul Tierney	2001–02	1	Retired

Few players in the history of United can ever have made such an instant impact as 'Kiko' Macheda. The Rome-born striker was spotted playing for hometown club Lazio and signed professional forms with United at the start of 2008–09. He was in prolific form that season for the junior sides, and as the campaign built up to its climax the manager decided to give him some experience of the big-game atmosphere, putting him on the bench against Aston Villa at Old Trafford on 5 April. With Liverpool breathing down United's necks, a win was vital to maintain a one-point gap at the top, but just before the hour-mark Villa went into a 2–1 lead. Sir Alex responded immediately by throwing on the Italian. Cristiano Ronaldo equalised, and the boss brought on Danny Welbeck for Carlos Tevez as he searched for the vital win. Three minutes into added time, Macheda received the ball on the edge of the box, turned and slammed it past Brad Friedel. The win proved crucial as United held on to their title.

BEST MONTHS FOR UNITED

	Month	P	W	D	L	Win %
1	January	572	294	124	154	51.40
2	May	183	94	44	45	51.37
3	February	496	249	122	125	50.20
4	September	651	323	160	168	49.62
5	December	623	306	136	181	49.12
6	October	575	280	138	157	48.70
7	November	519	248	123	148	47.78
8	April	700	334	168	198	47.71
9	August	300	140	83	77	46.67
10	March	606	277	149	180	45.71

Sir Alex Ferguson has often said that United get stronger as the season builds up to its climax, and the three best months for the Reds all fall in the second half of the campaign. In recent years, the best May undoubtedly came in 2008 when United emerged victorious in all their games – even though one of the matches is officially recorded as a draw. At the start of the month, United and Chelsea were level on points in the title race, but the Reds had a vastly superior goal difference. First up were West Ham at Old Trafford. Goals from Cristiano Ronaldo (2) and a stunning 30-yard drive from Carlos Tevez inside the first 30 minutes put United in control. Then came a trip to Wigan where, amid thunder and lightning, United secured a 2–0 win and a 17th league title. Then came the big one: the Champions League final against Chelsea in Moscow's Luzhniki Stadium. The game ended in a 1–1 draw, Ronaldo almost inevitably scoring, but we all know who won the penalty shoot-out.

GEORGE BEST'S ALL-TIME UNITED XI

	Player	Career	Appearances	Goals
1	Harry Gregg	1957–66	247	0
2	**Viv Anderson**	1987–90	69	4
3	Johnny Carey	1937–53	344	17
4	Martin Buchan	1972–82	456	4
5	Roger Byrne	1951–58	280	20
6	Duncan Edwards	1953–58	177	21
7	Bryan Robson	1981–94	461	99
8	Pat Crerand	1963–71	397	15
9	Bobby Charlton	1956–73	758	249
10	Eric Cantona	1992–97	185	82
11	Denis Law	1962–73	404	237

Asked in 1996 to pick his all-time United XI, George Best selected the above side, with Sir Matt Busby as manager and Steve Bruce, Ryan Giggs, Andrei Kanchelskis and Dennis Viollet making it to the bench. Arguably the most surprising choice of the lot is Viv Anderson, not through any lack of quality as a full-back, but because his career at United was so short. When he arrived at United, he was almost 31 and had already won the European Cup twice with Nottingham Forest and further honours at Arsenal. But his significance is shown by the fact that, along with Brian McClair, he was Alex Ferguson's first signing at United. Apart from the 30 England caps Anderson won, the reason the manager wanted him was his 'resolute professionalism . . . and bubbly, contagious enthusiasm in the dressing-room'. Anderson was an early sign of what the new era at United would be like. In January 1991 he left on a free transfer to Sheffield Wednesday.

MOST FA CUP SEMI-FINALS

	Team	Last Appearance	Total
1	Manchester United	2011	27
2	Arsenal	2009	26
3	Everton	2009	24
4	Liverpool	2006	22
5	Aston Villa	2010	20
5	West Bromwich Albion	2008	20
7	Chelsea	2010	19
8	Blackburn Rovers	2007	18
8	Tottenham Hotspur	2010	18
10	Newcastle United	2005	17

By reaching the semi-final in 2011, United set a new record as the first team to reach this stage of the FA Cup 27 times. Perhaps one of the most vital semi-finals came in April 1990. That season, Alex Ferguson's expensively acquired side had struggled to find consistency and ended the campaign in a disappointing 13th place – the worst league finish in his time at the club. The route to Wembley provided an opportunity for salvation, and standing in United's way were Oldham Athletic, then mid-table in the Second Division. But the Reds didn't have it all their own way and nearly succumbed to the underdogs. Bryan Robson, Neil Webb and Danny Wallace all scored for United, while Oldham's goalscorers were Earl Barrett, Ian Marshall and Roger Palmer in a compelling 3–3 draw. In the replay at Maine Road three days later, United edged home thanks to a winner from 20-year-old Mark Robins running on to a pass from Mike Phelan. After another replay, United won the final and Ferguson had his first trophy at United – and everything changed.

UNITED'S PLAYERS FROM LATIN AMERICA

	Player	Country	Debut	Apps (Goals)
1	Juan Sebastian Veron	Argentina	19 August 2001	82 (11)
2	Diego Forlan	Uruguay	29 January 2002	98 (17)
3	Kleberson	Brazil	27 August 2003	30 (2)
4	Gabriel Heinze	Argentina	11 September 2004	83 (4)
5	Carlos Tevez	Argentina	15 August 2007	99 (34)
6	Anderson	Brazil	1 September 2007	129 (5)
7	Rafael da Silva	Brazil	17 August 2008	72 (2)
7	Rodrigo Possebon	Brazil	17 August 2008	8 (0)
9	Fabio da Silva	Brazil	24 January 2009	38 (2)
10	Antonio Valencia	Ecuador	9 August 2009	69 (10)
11	Javier Hernandez	Mexico	8 August 2010	45 (20)

It wasn't until early in the 21st century that United began to recruit players from Latin America, a generation after the likes of Ossie Ardiles and Ricky Villa had blazed a trail in English football. However, the first player from that region to make more than 100 appearances for the Reds was Anderson, or, to give him his full name, Anderson Luis de Abreu Oliveira. Having begun his career with Gremio in Brazil, he moved to Porto early in 2006, before joining United at the start of the 2007–08 campaign. Born in Brazil on 13 April 1988, his progress has been interrupted by injury problems, but the all-action midfielder still managed to make a very late substitute appearance in the Champions League final in 2008, and scored from the penalty spot in the shoot-out that decided the tie in United's favour. Given his goalscoring record, it was a brave move to step forward, but he remained calm under the most intense pressure. He finally scored for United on his 76th appearance for the Reds, against Spurs in September 2009.

MOST APPEARANCES IN THE
FIRST DIVISION

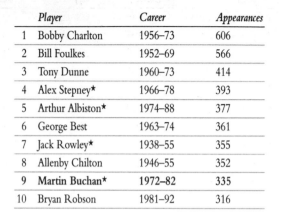

	Player	Career	Appearances
1	Bobby Charlton	1956–73	606
2	Bill Foulkes	1952–69	566
3	Tony Dunne	1960–73	414
4	Alex Stepney★	1966–78	393
5	Arthur Albiston★	1974–88	377
6	George Best	1963–74	361
7	Jack Rowley★	1938–55	355
8	Allenby Chilton	1946–55	352
9	**Martin Buchan★**	**1972–82**	**335**
10	Bryan Robson	1981–92	316

In Frank O'Farrell's brief tenure as United manager, there is no doubt as to who was his most significant signing: Martin Buchan. He was bought from Aberdeen in February 1972 for a fee of £135,000. Aged just 22 at the time, Buchan had already made his Scotland debut that season and had been his club captain for a couple of years. He was a calm, classy and authoritative central defender who soon became United's captain. Pace was arguably his most vital asset, and he had a thunderous shot on him (put to use in a famous strike against Everton in September 1978), though his goals came very rarely. Although he would be high on many fans' list of best defenders the club has ever had, he won just one major honour: the 1977 FA Cup, when he became the only man to captain sides to victory in both the FA Cup and the Scottish Cup (Aberdeen in 1970). Latterly, his career was somewhat blighted by injury, and eventually he left the club for Oldham Athletic.

★These players each spent one season in Division Two.

MOST GOALS IN THE FIRST DIVISION

	Player	Career	Appearances	Goals
1	Bobby Charlton	1956–73	606	199
2	Jack Rowley★	1938–55	355	173
3	Denis Law	1962–73	309	171
4	Dennis Viollet	1953–61	259	159
5	George Best	1963–74	361	137
6	Stan Pearson★	1938–53	301	125
7	David Herd	1961–68	202	114
8	Tommy Taylor	1953–58	166	112
9	Joe Spence†	1919–31	312	106
10	Sandy Turnbull	1907–15	220	90

It took Denis Law just 139 league games, and a little over four seasons, to score 100 goals for United in the First Division. He didn't have to wait long to get onto the scoresheet after his record transfer to the club: he hit home from Johnny Giles' cross early in his debut on 18 August 1962 against West Bromwich Albion at Old Trafford. But surprisingly it was another seven games before he was back on target – such fallow periods were very rare in his career – a reflection of the team's difficulties that year. Although the club finished 19th out of 22 in his first season, he still ended the campaign with 23 league goals – a strike rate that arguably kept the team from relegation. He followed up with 30 goals the next season and then 28 in 1964–65, helping United to the league title. After that, as injuries increasingly took their toll, he managed 20-plus league goals in a season only once more, in 1966–67, and it was no coincidence that United were once again league champions.

★These players spent one season in Division Two.
†He spent four seasons in Division Two.

GARY NEVILLE'S GREATEST MOMENTS

	Opposition	Date	Competition	Result
1	Crystal Palace	5 May 1992	Youth Cup final	6–3 (agg)
2	Torpedo Moscow	16 September 1992	UEFA Cup 1st	0–0
3	Middlesbrough	5 May 1996	Premier League	3–0
4	Liverpool	11 May 1996	FA Cup final	1–0
5	Arsenal	14 April 1999	FA Cup semi-final R	2–1
6	Juventus	21 April 1999	Champions Lg SF	3–2
7	Bayern Munich	26 May 1999	Champions Lg final	2–1
8	Wigan Athletic	26 February 2006	League Cup final	4–0
9	West Ham United	13 May 2007	Premier League	0–1
10	Stoke City	24 October 2010	Premier League	2–1

Picking ten memorable games out of more than 600 for United is quite a task, but Gary Neville lists these as the ones that mean the most. The Youth Cup win of 1992 is an early highlight: 'We were the best of friends, and a lot of us still are. There's a spirit from that incredible team that'll live forever.' Four months later, he made his senior debut: 'I remember going home that night and thinking: "If I die tonight, I die happy." That was probably my greatest achievement because I had realised my dream of playing for United at Old Trafford and nobody could ever take that away from me.' Then came a run of trophies, but the 1999 FA Cup semi-final still stands out: 'That Arsenal team between 1997 and 1999 were the best domestic team I ever faced, and the FA Cup semi-final replay against them was the best game I have ever played in.' Soon after was that remarkable Champions League final: 'I just lay on the floor thinking: "Oh my God, we've done it".'

MOST COMMON SURNAMES

	Surname	Players	Total
1	Jones	David (1937), David (2004), Mark, Owen, Peter, Richard, Tom, Tommy	8
2	Davies	Alan, Joe, John, L., Ron, Simon, Wyn	7
2	Smith	Alan, Albert, Dick, Jack, Lawrence, Tom, William	7
2	Williams	Bill, Frank, Fred, Harry (1900), Harry (1920), Joe, Rees	7
5	Anderson	Anderson, George, John, Trevor, Viv, Willie	6
5	Brown	James (1892), James (1932), James (1935), Robert, Wes, William	6
7	Gibson	Colin, Darron, Don, Richard, Terry	5
7	Owen	Bill, George, Jack, Michael, W.	5
7	Wilson	David, Edgar, Jack, Mark, Tommy	5

United have always kept up with the Joneses – and everyone else, for that matter. Of the eight players to share that surname, only Tom Jones (who made 200 appearances without ever scoring in the 1920s) and Mark Jones have had long careers at United. A ninth Jones, England Under-21 international Phil, joined the club from Blackburn Rovers during the summer of 2011 and will hope to add to that list. But Mark's place in the club's history is a hugely significant one. Born near Barnsley in Yorkshire in 1933, he escaped working in the mines when he was signed up by United after leaving school. He made his debut at 17 and was a big (6ft 1in), tough central defender, naturally strong in the air. However, it wasn't until 1955–56 that he became a regular in the side, playing every game in United's title-winning campaign. He was often in competition with Jackie Blanchflower, a more flexible and skilful player, for the centre-half position. Both were on the fateful flight back from Belgrade on 6 February 1958, and Jones was one of the eight tragic fatal victims from that glorious team.

HIGHEST ATTENDANCES FOR UNITED
AT OLD TRAFFORD

	Opposition	Date	Score	Attendance
1	Blackburn Rovers	31 March 2007	4–1	76,098
2	Aston Villa	13 January 2007	3–1	76,073
3	Bolton Wanderers	17 March 2007	4–1	76,058
4	Watford	31 January 2007	4–0	76,032
5	Wigan Athletic	26 December 2006	3–1	76,018
6	West Ham United	3 May 2008	4–1	76,013
7	Portsmouth	4 November 2006	3–0	76,004
8	Liverpool	23 March 2008	3–0	76,000
9	Arsenal	13 April 2008	2–1	75,985
10	Manchester City	10 February 2008	1–2	75,970

All the above games were Premier League fixtures, and after the 2007–08 season the capacity at Old Trafford was slightly reduced, so the record set on 31 March 2007 should stand for a while yet. United had been leading the title race for much of the season, but after an international break and with a Champions League tie in Rome scheduled for the following midweek, the visit of Rovers was always going to be a tough challenge. So it proved in the first half when the Lancashire side took the lead, and things went from bad to worse when Nemanja Vidic picked up a serious shoulder injury. But Paul Scholes was in inspired form and drew United level after 61 minutes. Sniffing victory, United then followed with goals from Michael Carrick, Ji-Sung Park and Ole Gunnar Solskjaer (his last for the club). Sir Alex Ferguson highlighted the key turning point in the match: 'I think it was a performance of champions, but Scholes' goal is what won us the game.'

UNITED'S GAMES ON 29 FEBRUARY

	Opponents	Year	Score	Competition
1	Burton Wanderers	1896	1–2	Div 2
2	Birmingham City	1908	1–0	Div 1
3	Reading	1912	3–0	FA Cup 3rd R
4	Blackpool	1936	3–2	Div 2
5	Sunderland	1964	3–3	FA Cup 6th
6	Middlesbrough	1972	3–0	FA Cup 5th R
7	Coventry City	1992	0–0	Div 1

There have been a possible 30 occasions on which United could have played a fixture on 'Leap Day', and the Reds have an impressive unbeaten record on that day dating back 115 years. United's last fixture on this day was a scarcely memorable 0–0 draw at Highfield Road where relegation candidates Coventry City held off the Reds' challenge so that at the end of the day Leeds had closed to within two points of United in the title race. The game did provide a rare outing that season for keeper Gary Walsh. The Wigan-born goalie had made his United debut as long ago as December 1986, when he was just 18. Just six weeks into his reign, it was an early example of Alex Ferguson trusting in youth. At the time, Walsh looked a natural and many thought he might go on to be one of the all-time greats, until he picked up some injuries that knocked back his progress. The arrival first of Jim Leighton and then Peter Schmeichel meant he was down the pecking order. His most regular spell of first-team action was for Bradford City, when he formed part of the side that appeared in the Premier League for two seasons.

ENGLAND CAPTAINS TO HAVE PLAYED FOR UNITED

	Player	Period	Games	At United
1	Bobby Charlton	1969–70	3	3
2	Ray Wilkins	1982–86	10	2
3	Bryan Robson	1982–91	65	65
4	Paul Ince	1993–98	7	2
5	David Beckham	2000–08	59	24
6	Michael Owen	2002–05	8	0
7	**Rio Ferdinand**	**2008–10**	**7**	**7**
8	Wayne Rooney	2009	1	1

Rio Ferdinand is the most recent United player to have captained England, last doing so on 30 May 2010 before injury deprived him of the armband. On 4 June 2011, he won his 81st cap for his country in the European Championship qualifier against Switzerland. The central defender has been one of the most consistent performers for United since joining the club from Leeds in the summer of 2002. His transfer fee was a world record for a defender, at about £30 million, but over the last nine seasons and 360 appearances he has gone on to justify the faith shown in him by Sir Alex Ferguson. A calm, assured figure at the back, he is also one of the most skilful ball-players in that role, while his reading of the game means that he rarely seems hurried. While at United, he has had a range of defensive allies, but it is his partnership with Nemanja Vidic since early in 2006 that has formed the bedrock of four title-winning sides and taken the Reds to three Champions League finals. The Peckham-born defender has done much charity work over the years to help keep people from similarly deprived areas away from trouble.

FIRST INTERNATIONALS TO PLAY
FOR THE CLUB

	Player	Country	First Cap	Caps (Goals)*
1	Tom Burke	Wales	26 February 1887	3
1	Jack Powell	Wales	26 February 1887	5
3	Jack Doughty	Wales	12 March 1887	7 (6)
4	Jos Davies	Wales	4 February 1888	5
5	Roger Doughty	Wales	3 March 1888	2 (2)
6	George Owen	Wales	15 April 1889	2 (2)
7	Jack Owen	Wales	5 March 1892	1
8	Caesar Jenkyns	Wales	6 March 1897	1 (1)
9	Charlie Roberts	England	25 February 1905	3
10	Billy Meredith	Wales	23 February 1907	26 (3)
11	George Wall	England	18 March 1907	7 (2)
12	Harold Halse	England	1 June 1909	1 (2)
13	Mickey Hamill	Ireland	10 February 1912	3 (1)
14	Alex Bell	Scotland	16 March 1912	1

As this list shows, in United's early Newton Heath days the club
had strong links with Wales. On 3 March 1888 Jos Davies, Jack and
Roger Doughty and Jack Powell all lined up for their country as
they took on Ireland at Wrexham's Racecourse Ground. The result
was a record win for the home side, who beat Ireland 11–0, with
Jack Doughty scoring four times and Roger Doughty twice. None
of the four players was still with the Heathens when they joined the
Football League in 1892, and the club had to wait until 1897 to
field an international while part of the league, when Caesar Jenkyns
played for Wales.

*While at Newton Heath/Manchester United.

MOST APPEARANCES FOR GOALKEEPERS

	Player	Career	Appearances
1	Alex Stepney	1966–78	539
2	Peter Schmeichel	1991–99	398
3	Gary Bailey	1978–87	375
4	Alfred Steward	1920–32	326
5	Harry Moger	1903–12	266
5	Edwin van der Sar	2005–11	266
7	Harry Gregg	1957–66	247
8	Jack Crompton	1946–55	212
9	Ray Wood	1949–58	208
10	Jack Mew	1912–26	199

Arguably United's greatest-ever keeper, Peter Schmeichel was once described by *Shoot!* as 'the most famous giant blond Dane since Brigitte Nielsen'. He was signed from Danish club Brondby in August 1991 for the bargain fee of £500,000 – Alex Ferguson called it 'the buy of the century'. At 27, he was still learning his skills. But any gaps in his armoury were soon eradicated: he dominated the box, intimidated any strikers bearing down on goal, and was a pioneer in the way he distributed the ball to set up many counter-attacks ('like Glenn Hoddle's passes', said the boss). Having announced his plan to quit Old Trafford after the 1998–99 season, he ensured it ended in the perfect Treble. While everyone remembers Ryan Giggs' goal to win the FA Cup semi-final, Schmeichel's previous penalty save from Dennis Bergkamp often gets overlooked. And of course, Schmeichel was in the opposition penalty area causing trouble when United scored their late equaliser in the Champions League final against Bayern Munich. Lifting the trophy as captain after that match was a fitting finale.

BIGGEST AWAY WINS

	Opposition	Venue	Date	Comp	Score
1	Nottingham Forest	City Ground	6 February 1999	PL	8–1
2	Grimsby Town	Blundell Park	26 December 1899	Div 2	7–0
3	Northampton Town	County Ground	7 February 1970	FAC 5	8–2
4	Chesterfield	Saltergate	13 November 1937	Div 2	7–1
5	Shamrock Rovers	Dalymount Park	25 September 1957	EC PR	6–0
5	Blackpool	Bloomfield Road	27 February 1960	Div 1	6–0
5	**Bolton Wanderers**	**Burnden Park**	**25 February 1996**	**PL**	**6–0**
8	Ipswich Town	Portman Road	3 September 1963	Div 1	7–2

United's 6–0 thrashing of Bolton saw the Reds close to within four points of Newcastle United, having played a game more, as the title run-in began in earnest. With their next fixture a visit to St James' Park, it sent out a chilling message to Kevin Keegan's men: we want our title back. It was the first time United had met Bolton in the league in 16 years, and a 21,381 capacity crowd was looking forward to the game. For the United fans among them at least, it was a great day. The first goal came after a superb run and lob by Ryan Giggs that hit the bar and was followed in by David Beckham. Steve Bruce then headed home a Beckham corner. In the second half, Andrew Cole rammed one past Trotters keeper Keith Branagan, then substitute Paul Scholes added two more before Nicky Butt completed the rout in stoppage time from Cole's pass. At the beginning of the season, Alan Hansen had famously questioned whether United could win anything with kids; this victory showed that the kids (Phil Neville also played that day) would be all right – even in a potentially tricky derby match such as this.

MOST APPEARANCES WITHOUT SCORING

	Player	Career	Appearances
1	Charlie Moore	1919–30	328
2	Tom Jones	1924–35	200
3	Jack Mellor	1930–36	122
4	Mal Donaghy	1988–92	119
5	Dick Holden	1905–12	117
6	Don Gibson	1950–55	115
7	George Perrins	1892–96	102
8	Jeff Whitefoot	1950–56	95
9	George Roughton	1936–39	92
10	Jonny Evans	2007–	86

The inter-war period was the time when United not only struggled to win matches, but often also struggled to score goals. Perhaps this wasn't so surprising when the two players with the longest careers without scoring played together for much of that time. Charlie Moore made his United debut on 30 August 1919 in the 1–1 draw at Derby County in the first game after the break for World War One. He partnered Tom Jones at full-back for the first time on 8 November 1924 in another 1–1 draw, this time against Portsmouth. All told, they played together 54 times in their careers, and, with two such blockers in action, it wasn't surprising that on 22 of those occasions United failed to score. Their last pairing came on 18 January 1930 when 21,028 turned up at Old Trafford in the hope of finally seeing a goal from either man – but United lost 3–0 to Middlesbrough. The reason they didn't play together more often was that they were battling with Jack Silcock for a full-back berth. He was comparatively prolific, with two goals in 449 appearances!

RYAN GIGGS' LEAGUE APPEARANCE LANDMARKS

Appearance	Opposition	Venue	Date	Score
1st	Everton	H	2 March 1991	0–2
100th	Aston Villa	H	19 December 1993	3–1
200th	Wimbledon	H	29 January 1997	2–1 (1 goal)
300th	Coventry City	A	4 November 2000	2–1
400th	Bolton Wanderers	A	7 January 2004	2–1
500th	Sheffield United	H	17 April 2007	2–0
600th	Tottenham Hotspur	A	16 January 2011	0–0
607th	Liverpool	A	6 March 2011	1–3
613th	Blackburn Rovers	A	14 May 2011	1–1

When Ryan Giggs made his league debut, coming on as a substitute for Denis Irwin, he was only 17 years and 93 days old and Kenny Dalglish had just resigned as manager of champions Liverpool. It was not an auspicious start, as mid-table Everton won, but he made up for that by scoring on his starting debut later that season, against local rivals City. Few could have imagined they were witnessing the start of a career at United that would last for more than 20 years. Eventually, he broke all major appearance records for the club. Ahead of his 600th league appearance, Sir Alex Ferguson, who had managed him throughout his entire career, commented on the current form and achievements of the 37-year-old: 'Ryan is an incredible human being. His fitness was fantastic. He has been doing that for two decades. He is an amazing man.' When Giggs played his 607th league game for United, he broke Bobby Charlton's club record of 606. His 613th not only marked the day the Reds secured their record 19th league title, but was also the occasion he broke David James' Premier League record of 572 appearances.

MOST APPEARANCES FOR
DAVE SEXTON'S SIGNINGS

	Player	Career	Appearances	Goals
1	Gary Bailey	1978–87	375	0
2	**Kevin Moran**	**1978–88**	**289**	**24**
3	Gordon McQueen	1978–85	229	26
4	Ray Wilkins	1979–84	194	10
5	Joe Jordan	1978–81	126	41
6	Mickey Thomas	1978–81	110	15
7	Garry Birtles	1980–82	64	12
8	Nikola Jovanovic	1980–81	26	4
9	Tom Sloan	1978–80	12	0
10	Tom Connell	1978	2	0

Kevin Moran's background in Gaelic football arguably came in handy for this fearless central defender, who regularly put his head where the boots were flying and has the scars to prove it. He made his debut away at Southampton late in the 1978–79 season, and played for United for nine years before moving to Sporting Gijon on a free transfer, and then coming back to England to play for Blackburn Rovers until he was 38. At his testimonial in August 1988, George Best notoriously failed to turn up. Moran went to the same school in Dublin, Drimnagh Castle, as fellow Republic of Ireland internationals Niall Quinn and Gerry Ryan, who came on as a substitute against Moran for Brighton in the 1983 FA Cup final. Sadly for Moran, it is for being the first man ever sent off in an FA Cup final, in 1985 after a foul on Everton's Peter Reid, that he earned his place in the record books. Despite being reduced to ten men, United still won the game 1–0.

MOST LEAGUE DOUBLES

	Team	First Time	Most Recent	Total
1	Aston Villa	1947–48	2007–08	16
1	Everton	1907–08	2007–08	16
3	Arsenal	1902–03	2009–10	15
3	Tottenham Hotspur	1952–53	2009–10	15
5	Manchester City	1894–95	2009–10	14
6	Blackpool	1897–98	2010–11	13
6	Bolton Wanderers	1909–10	2009–10	13
6	Chelsea	1907–08	1987–88	13
6	Leicester City	1903–04	2003–04	13
6	Middlesbrough	1900–01	2008–09	13

United have a great track record against the Blue half of Merseyside, at one stage achieving four successive Premier League doubles over the Toffees between 2000–01 and 2003–04. In 2002–03, the six points United gained from Everton made all the difference in the title race with Arsenal. The Gunners had been champions the year before, while United had slipped down to third in the table. The Old Trafford encounter on 7 October ended 3–0 to the Reds, but with 85 minutes on the clock it was still 0–0 and United's stuttering start to regain the title looked likely to continue. But Paul Scholes capped an excellent performance by scoring with less than five minutes remaining, after a cross from Ryan Giggs was half cleared, and then added his second with a fierce shot, while Ruud van Nistelrooy converted a penalty. After a 17-match unbeaten run that had taken them to the top of the table, United went to Goodison Park for the last game of the season knowing they were champions and duly won 2–1, despite going behind to an early goal.

UNITED'S FIRST MILLION-POUND SIGNINGS

	Player	Career	Appearances	Goals	Fee
1	Bryan Robson	1981–94	461	99	£1.5 million
2	Mark Hughes*	1983–95	467	163	£1.8 million
3	Neil Webb	1989–92	110	11	£1.5 million
4	Gary Pallister	1989–98	437	15	£2.3 million
5	Paul Ince	1989–95	281	29	£2.4 million
6	Danny Wallace	1989–93	71	11	£1.3 million
7	Andrei Kanchelskis	1991–95	161	36	£1.0 million
8	**Paul Parker**	**1991–96**	**146**	**2**	**£1.7 million**
9	Dion Dublin	1992–94	17	3	£1.0 million
10	Eric Cantona	1992–97	185	82	£1.0 million

The United side that won the Premier League in 1993 and 1994 featured a defence all of whom had been bought by Alex Ferguson. Peter Schmeichel, Denis Irwin and Steve Bruce had each cost under a million, but Gary Pallister and right-back Paul Parker topped that level. Together, they formed the strong base for the rest of the side. Parker was 27 when he arrived at United from QPR, but it was his performances for England during the 1990 World Cup that brought him to wider notice. His boyhood team Spurs were also keen to sign him, but when he visited Old Trafford in July he realised he had to come to United – it wasn't the money, but the fact the place was buzzing even then. As well as the two league titles, he also won the League Cup in 1992 and the FA Cup in 1994. Thereafter, knee problems and the rise of Gary Neville meant that his opportunities at United were limited, and he moved to Derby in 1996.

*Mark Hughes had played for United from 1983–86 before being sold to Barcelona and then bought back in 1988.

PREMIER LEAGUE TITLES

	Season	P	W	D	L	F	A	Pts
1	1992–93	42	24	12	6	67	31	84
2	1993–94	42	27	11	4	80	38	92
3	1995–96	38	25	7	6	73	35	82
4	1996–97	38	21	12	5	76	44	75
5	1998–99	38	22	13	3	80	37	79
6	1999–2000	38	28	7	3	97	45	91
7	2000–01	38	24	8	6	79	31	80
8	2002–03	38	25	8	5	74	34	83
9	2006–07	38	28	5	5	83	27	89
10	2007–08	38	27	6	5	80	22	87
11	2008–09	38	28	6	4	68	24	90
12	2010–11	38	23	11	4	78	37	80

In the first 19 years of the Premier League, United have won the title 12 times – each occasion being special for some reason. But perhaps the most significant win came in 1992–93 as the Reds ended a 26-year wait for the title. The previous season, United had slipped up at the end to allow Leeds United to snatch the trophy. There was only one significant new recruit to the squad that year – Eric Cantona – but he brought a new level of creativity and confidence to the side, though the team also had the best defensive record in the league. There were some tense moments along the way, but this time United finished the campaign with seven straight wins to end up champions by ten clear points. They clinched the trophy when their nearest challengers, Aston Villa, lost on May Day, leaving United's last two games to become victory processions.

MOST APPEARANCES FOR UNITED BY IRISH PLAYERS

	Player	Career	Appearances
1	Tony Dunne	1960–73	535
2	Denis Irwin	1990–2002	529
3	Roy Keane	1993–2005	480
4	George Best	1963–74	470
5	Sammy McIlroy	1971–82	419
6	**John O'Shea**	**1999–2011**	**393**
7	Shay Brennan	1958–70	359
8	Johnny Carey	1937–53	344
9	Kevin Moran	1979–88	289
10	Frank Stapleton	1981–87	288

In 2011, John O'Shea picked up his fifth Premier League winner's medal since he joined the club as an apprentice, having been spotted by United's scouts while playing in his home town of Waterford. One of the most versatile players in the modern game, he mostly appeared at full-back, but was also at home in the midfield or at centre-back – and even took over the gloves to go in goal in February 2007 against Spurs, when Edwin van der Sar had to go off with a broken nose. He began to feature regularly in the United line-up in 2002–03, but his versatility has meant he often started from the bench – only Ole Gunnar Solskjaer, Ryan Giggs and Paul Scholes have registered more substitute appearances. This meant he ended up being an unused substitute in the 2008 Champions League final, though in the following year's final he started at right-back against Barcelona. That season he was also part of the defence that clocked up 14 successive clean sheets. In July 2011, he signed for Sunderland.

MOST GOALS FOR UNITED
BY IRISH PLAYERS

	Player	Career	Goals
1	George Best	1963–74	179
2	Frank Stapleton	1981–87	78
3	Sammy McIlroy	1971–82	71
4	Norman Whiteside	1982–89	67
5	Billy Whelan	1955–58	52
6	Roy Keane	1993–2005	51
7	Denis Irwin	1990–2002	33
8	Gerry Daly	1973–77	32
9	Jackie Blanchflower	1951–57	27
10	Kevin Moran	1979–88	24

There are many reasons why the Reds have such a strong following in Ireland: Irish emigrants moving to the city; the legacy of
Munich; and United's inspirational Irish captains, such as Johnny
Carey and Roy Keane. But the biggest reason can be summed up
in two words: George Best. As a young teenager, Best played for
Cregagh in his native Belfast, and the coach of the side, Bud
McFarlane, tipped off United's local scout Bob Bishop that Best
could be special. He was. Sent over to Manchester, he made his
debut in September 1963, aged 17, and before the year was out had
scored the first of his 179 goals, against Burnley. The following
season he missed just one of United's 60 games, scoring 14 goals.
Already, at 18, he had become central to everything United did. In
1967–68, his most prolific campaign, he scored 32 goals, helped
United to the European Cup and was unsurprisingly chosen as
European Footballer of the Year. It was the first of five successive
seasons when he was United's leading goalscorer in the league.

FIRST UNITED PLAYERS IN
WORLD CUP FINALS

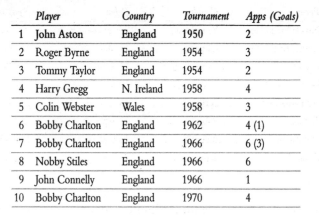

	Player	Country	Tournament	Apps (Goals)
1	John Aston	England	1950	2
2	Roger Byrne	England	1954	3
3	Tommy Taylor	England	1954	2
4	Harry Gregg	N. Ireland	1958	4
5	Colin Webster	Wales	1958	3
6	Bobby Charlton	England	1962	4 (1)
7	Bobby Charlton	England	1966	6 (3)
8	Nobby Stiles	England	1966	6
9	John Connelly	England	1966	1
10	Bobby Charlton	England	1970	4

John Aston Sr was the first United player ever to appear in the World Cup. The left-back played against Chile, when England won 2–0, but was left out of the side after the notorious 1–0 defeat to the United States. Aston was born in Prestbury and was signed by United in 1939, but the war intervened before he could make his debut. He served as a Royal Marine in the Middle East, before returning to United where new manager Matt Busby soon converted him to play at full-back rather than as a forward. Just how useful he was in the latter role was shown when he had to step in as centre-forward during the 1950–51 season, scoring 15 goals in 26 appearances. A skilful, energetic defender, his most famous role was to mark Stanley Matthews in the 1948 FA Cup final, helping ensure United won 4–2. In 1954, he was diagnosed with tuberculosis, which brought his playing career to an end, though he later became a coach and scout for United.

PLAYERS FROM BEHIND THE 'IRON CURTAIN'

	Player	Country	Debut	Apps (Goals)
1	Nikola Jovanovic	Yugoslavia	2 February 1980	26 (4)
2	Andrei Kanchelskis	Ukraine	11 May 1991	161 (36)
3	Karel Poborsky	Czech Republic	11 August 1996	48 (6)
4	Bojan Djordjic	Serbia	19 May 2001	2
5	Nemanja Vidic	Serbia	25 January 2006	233 (18)
6	Tomasz Kuszczak	Poland	17 September 2006	61
7	Dimitar Berbatov	Bulgaria	13 September 2008	128 (47)
8	Zoran Tosic	Serbia	24 January 2009	5

Of all the players to have joined United from the other side of the old Iron Curtain, none has had such a huge impact as Nemanja Vidic. The Serbian defender had begun his career at Red Star Belgrade, before moving to Spartak Moscow. Fans did not realise it at the time, but they got one of their best Christmas presents in 2005 when United announced he would be signing for the club. It was a rare mid-season foray into the transfer market for Sir Alex, but a vital one. Within a few weeks of arriving, Vidic had picked up his first trophy at United (the Carling Cup) and soon formed one of the club's all-time great defensive partnerships with Rio Ferdinand. The bedrock of four Premier League title-winning sides, he is one of the most committed and fearless defenders you could wish for, dominant in the air in both boxes. During the 2010–11 campaign, he was Sir Alex's most regular pick in the Premier League, making 35 starting appearances, as the club secured a record 19th league title. Early in the season, he was appointed club captain and commented: 'I'm very happy with it. It is a major responsibility but I have always liked responsibility.'

YOUTH CUP VICTORIES

	Opponent	Year	Score*
1	Wolverhampton Wanderers	1953	9–3
2	Wolverhampton Wanderers	1954	5–4
3	West Bromwich Albion	1955	7–1
4	Chesterfield	1956	4–3
5	West Ham United	1957	8–2
6	Swindon Town	1964	5–2
7	Crystal Palace	1992	6–3
8	Tottenham Hotspur	1995	1–1 (won 4–2 on penalties)
9	Middlesbrough	2003	3–1
10	Sheffield United	2011	6–3

No club has won the Youth Cup more often than United's ten times (Arsenal are second with seven). Some great names have won the trophy: Duncan Edwards (1953–55), Bobby Charlton (1954–56), George Best (1964), David Beckham and Ryan Giggs (1992) are just a few of the Reds' most famous Youth Cup winners. Since just before the Second World War, the club had focused on bringing in the best young talent, and so the creation of the Youth Cup in 1952–53 was a perfect opportunity to show what they could do. Matt Busby and Jimmy Murphy (who managed the youth side) saw it as a way to instil a love of United and the right virtues into players at the earliest stage. When they reached the first final, United had three players – Edwards, Eddie Lewis and David Pegg – who had made their first-team debuts that season, and seven others, including Eddie Colman, Albert Scanlon and Billy Whelan, who would achieve that honour subsequently. After winning the first leg 7–1, they eased off to draw the second 2–2.

*The Youth Cup final is played over two legs, home and away.

MOST APPEARANCES IN THE EUROPA LEAGUE★

	Player	Career	Appearances
1	Arthur Albiston	1974–88	15
2	**Gary Bailey**	**1978–87**	**12**
3	George Best	1963–74	11
3	Shay Brennan	1958–70	11
3	Bobby Charlton	1956–73	11
3	John Connelly	1964–66	11
3	Pat Crerand	1963–71	11
3	Pat Dunne	1964–65	11
3	Tony Dunne	1960–73	11
3	Bill Foulkes	1952–69	11
3	David Herd	1961–68	11
3	Nobby Stiles	1960–71	11

The tournament now known as the Europa League has been through many name changes. In 1964–65, when ten of the above appeared in 11 games, it was known as the Inter-Cities' Fairs Cup. By the time Gary Bailey was playing, it was the UEFA Cup and United competed in it in 1980–81, 1982–83 (being knocked out in the first round both times) and in 1984–85, when Bailey was the keeper who faced United's first ever penalty shoot-out, in the quarter-finals. Born in Ipswich, Bailey's family moved to South Africa and it was while he was studying at Wits University (or Half-Wits University as his team-mates called it) that he decided to join United. He made his debut in November 1978, but his 375-game career with the Reds was effectively ended by a knee injury picked up while with England in the 1986 World Cup.

★Includes Inter-Cities' Fairs Cup and UEFA Cup; United are yet to appear in the new format Europa League.

ALEX FERGUSON'S ASSISTANTS

	Assistant	Appointed	Left
1	Archie Knox	November 1986	May 1991
2	Brian Kidd	August 1991	December 1998
3	Jim Ryan	December 1998	February 1999★
4	Steve McClaren	February 1999	July 2001
5	Jim Ryan	July 2001	June 2002
6	Carlos Queiroz	June 2002	June 2003
7	Walter Smith	March 2004	July 2004★
8	Carlos Queiroz	July 2004	July 2008
9	Mike Phelan	September 2008	

When you have been manager for 25 years, almost inevitably you end up working with a range of different assistants in that time. It shows the calibre of those who have held the position that three of them – McClaren, Smith and Queiroz – have subsequently gone on to manage national sides. Furthermore, like Brian Kidd before him, the Nelson-born Mike Phelan is a former United player. He was signed by Alex Ferguson from Norwich City in the summer of 1989 for £750,000, and could play in midfield or at full-back, winning one cap for England in 1989. After 146 appearances in five seasons, he was given a free transfer to West Brom. It wasn't until 1999 that he returned to United in a coaching capacity, gradually working his way up the ladder until he took over as Sir Alex's assistant in the autumn of 2008. Phelan explained how his working relationship with Sir Alex has developed: 'He feeds off success and also from a coaching or management point of view he backs you totally.'

★Temporary appointments.

MOST COMMON FA CUP OPPONENTS

	Opponent	Period	Times Met
1	Liverpool	1898–2011	16
2	Southampton	1897–2011	15
2	Tottenham Hotspur	1899–2009	15
4	Arsenal	1906–2011	14
4	Middlesbrough	1894–2007	14
6	Fulham	1905–2009	13
7	Aston Villa	1906–2008	12
7	Reading	1912–2007	12
9	Chelsea	1908–2007	11
9	Everton	1903–2009	11
9	Stoke City	1895–1972	11

United's third-round tie against Liverpool in 2011 meant that the Merseysiders were out on their own as the club's most frequent opposition in the tournament. The two rivals met in the semi-finals in 1979 and 1985, United winning through on both occasions after a replay. They have also met in two finals: 1977 and 1996, with the Red Devils victorious each time. The 1977 final saw United as the underdogs, as Liverpool chased a Treble. The previous year, United had lost the final and manager Tommy Docherty promised the fans United would be back. He was as good as his word. On a sunny afternoon, Liverpool made most of the running in a scoreless first half, with Alex Stepney making a key save just before the break. Early in the second half, Stuart Pearson scored for United after a long ball up to Jimmy Greenhoff was knocked on to him. Liverpool equalised through Jimmy Case, and then United got the decider after a Lou Macari shot spun off Greenhoff and into the net.

THE TEAM FOR THE FIRST FA CUP VICTORY

	Player	Career	Appearances	Goals
1	Harry Moger	1903–12	266	0
2	George Stacey	1907–15	270	9
3	Vince Hayes	1901–10	128	2
4	Dick Duckworth	1903–13	254	11
5	**Charlie Roberts**	**1904–13**	**302**	**23**
6	Alex Bell	1903–13	309	10
7	Billy Meredith	1907–21	335	36
8	Harold Halse	1908–12	125	56
9	Jimmy Turnbull	1907–10	78	45
10	Sandy Turnbull	1907–15	247	101
11	George Wall	1906–15	319	100

United reached their first FA Cup final in 1909, a year after winning their first league title. The game was played at Crystal Palace in front of a crowd of 71,401, and their opponents were Bristol City, who had finished above United in the table. Wearing a change strip of white shirts with a red V, United scored the only goal of a rather disappointing game midway through the first half. A Harold Halse shot cannoned off the crossbar and Sandy Turnbull, struggling with a knee injury, was there to hit home. The skipper that day was Charlie Roberts, United's first 'Captain Marvel'. Roberts had signed for United from Grimsby in 1904, and manager Ernest Mangnall knew he was getting an inspirational character who could motivate his team. He also became a founding figure in the creation of the Players' Union. It would not be until 1985 that another English captain would get to lift the FA Cup for United.

MANCHESTER THROUGH AND THROUGH

	Player	Debut	Appearances	Goals
1	Ravel Morrison	26 October 2010	1	0
2	Richard Eckersley	24 January 2009	4	0
3	**Danny Welbeck**	23 September 2008	24	5
4	Danny Simpson	26 September 2007	8	0
5	Adam Eckersley	26 October 2005	1	0
5	Richie Jones	26 October 2005	5	0
7	Phil Bardsley	3 December 2003	18	0
7	Paul Tierney	3 December 2003	1	0
9	Mark Lynch	18 March 2003	1	0
10	Danny Pugh	18 September 2002	7	0
11	Danny Webber	28 November 2000	3	0

The above list shows all those players born in Manchester and Salford who have made their United debut since the start of the new millennium. There is always special excitement at local talent coming through. Danny Welbeck is one of the brightest such prospects for a long time, and has already begun to make an impact. Born in Longsight on 26 November 1990, Welbeck signed his trainee contract in July 2007 and by the end of the season was being considered for the first-team squad. He had to wait until early in the next season to make his debut, against Middlesbrough in the League Cup. On 15 November, still aged 17, he scored his first senior goal with a stunning long-range strike in United's 5–0 Premier League thumping of Stoke. In 2010–11, he was loaned to Sunderland, and during that period impressed enough to earn an England debut. During the summer, he scored both England's goals in the UEFA Under-21 tournament.

MOST APPEARANCES IN THE PREMIER LEAGUE

	Player	PL Career	Appearances
1	Ryan Giggs	1992–	573
2	Paul Scholes	1994–2011	466
3	**Gary Neville**	**1994–2011**	**400**
4	Roy Keane	1993–2005	326
5	Denis Irwin	1992–2002	296
6	Nicky Butt	1992–2004	270
7	David Beckham	1995–2003	265
8	Phil Neville	1995–2005	263
9	John O'Shea	2001–2011	256
10	Peter Schmeichel	1992–99	252

The strong presence on this list of the 'Class of 92', United's superb Youth Cup-winning side of that season, shows just what an influence that group has had on the Reds' success in the Premier League era. Among those players was Gary Neville, who announced his retirement in February 2011. Along with Ryan Giggs and Paul Scholes, he had come up through the youth ranks and been a part of the United set-up since the dawn of the Premier League. One of the most consistent and best right-backs of the modern era, Neville was a Red through and through. Utterly dedicated to the cause and ready to throw his body on the line, he was renowned for bombing forward down the right flank, and with David Beckham proved a fearsome combination for any opponent at club and international level. Towards the latter stages of his career, having proudly taken on the role of club captain, he suffered several injuries. He bowed out at this level with a 2–1 win away to West Brom on New Year's Day, having made his debut way back in May 1994.

HAT-TRICKS IN THE CHAMPIONS LEAGUE*

	Player	Opponents	Date	Score
1	Dennis Viollet	Anderlecht (H)	26 September 1956	10–0
2	Tommy Taylor (4)	Anderlecht (H)	26 September 1956	10–0
3	John Connelly	HJK Helsinki (H)	6 October 1965	6–0
4	David Herd	ASK Vorwaerts (H)	1 December 1965	3–1
5	Denis Law	Waterford (A)	18 September 1968	3–1
6	Denis Law (4)	Waterford (H)	2 October 1968	7–1
7	Andrew Cole	Feyenoord (A)	5 November 1997	3–1
8	Andrew Cole	Anderlecht (H)	13 September 2000	5–1
9	**Wayne Rooney**	**Fenerbahce (H)**	**28 September 2004**	**6–2**
10	Ruud van Nistelrooy (4)	Sparta Prague (H)	3 November 2004	4–1
11	Michael Owen	Wolfsburg (A)	8 December 2009	3–1

Any hat-trick in the European Cup or Champions League is notable, but the one scored by Wayne Rooney in 2004 takes some beating. During the previous summer, Rooney had joined United from Everton for a world-record fee for a teenager. The 18-year-old's debut for the Reds had been delayed, as he had picked up an injury during England's summer campaign in Euro 2004. Sir Alex had tried to make things as 'ordinary as possible' for him to limit the enormous hype over his long-awaited debut. Rooney immediately undid all that work by scoring a stunning hat-trick that proved he was not going to be overawed by his new surroundings. He scored his first goal with a left-foot strike on 17 minutes; ten minutes later he beat his defender and then hit a searing right-foot shot into the corner of the goal. Then, early in the second half, he scored from a free kick from the edge of the box. Not a bad start.

*Includes European Cup.

TEAMS THAT HAVE CONCEDED MOST GOALS TO UNITED

	Opponent	Played	Goals Conceded	Average Goals
1	Arsenal	212	320	1.51
2	Aston Villa	176	318	1.81
3	Newcastle United	152	297	1.95
4	Tottenham Hotspur	174	278	1.60
5	Everton	182	269	1.48
6	Chelsea	161	260	1.61
7	Liverpool	182	252	1.38
8	**Leicester City**	**117**	**234**	**2.00**
9	Manchester City	159	233	1.47
10	Sunderland	131	228	1.74

Of all the teams in this list, Leicester City have the worst record against United, conceding an average of exactly two goals per match. United's highest-scoring performance against the Foxes came in January 1999, with Dwight Yorke (3), Andrew Cole (2) and Jaap Stam on the scoresheet in a 6–2 win at Filbert Street. On eight other occasions, United put five past the unfortunate Leicester keeper. However, the most important win against them came in the 1963 FA Cup final. United had struggled all season in the First Division and ended up in 19th place, narrowly avoiding relegation, while Leicester were fourth. Denis Law put United 1–0 up after 30 minutes from Paddy Crerand's pass, before David Herd added a second. City then pulled one back, but Herd was on hand to put the ball home with five minutes remaining after Gordon Banks surprisingly spilled a cross from Johnny Giles. Law and Herd were a prolific partnership; between them they scored an astonishing 247 goals in four seasons from 1962–63 to 1965–66.

FROM SCHMEICHEL TO VAN DER SAR

	Player	Debut	Last Game	Appearances
1	Mark Bosnich	1 August 1999★	15 April 2000	38
2	Raimond van der Gouw	14 August 1999★	5 November 2001	60
3	Nick Culkin	22 August 1999	22 August 1999	1
4	Massimo Taibi	11 September 1999	3 October 1999	4
5	Paul Rachubka	11 January 2000	17 March 2001	3
6	**Fabien Barthez**	**13 August 2000**	**23 April 2003**	**139**
7	Andy Goram	14 April 2001	13 May 2001	2
8	Roy Carroll	26 August 2001	21 May 2005	72
9	Ricardo	18 September 2002	19 April 2003	5
10	Tim Howard	10 August 2003	11 February 2006	77

When Peter Schmeichel left Manchester United at the end of the 1998–99 season, finding an adequate replacement was tough. Until the arrival of Edwin van der Sar in August 2005, ten options were tried out, but only Fabien Barthez made the position his own for a sustained period. Signed from Monaco in the summer of 2000 for a fee of £7.8 million, he joined after France had followed up their World Cup triumph in 1998 with the European Championship. Barthez was a big personality who initially seemed to thrive at Old Trafford. With a supermodel girlfriend in Linda Evangelista, the only question some had was whether they would take to the Manchester climate. Though relatively small for a keeper, he had superb reflexes, and indulged in often-successful psychological warfare with his opponents at penalties. Sadly his most famous ploy, trying to persuade West Ham's Paolo di Canio he had been given offside when the Italian was clear through on goal in an FA Cup game, didn't work.

★Both these players appeared for United before these dates, Bosnich in a previous spell at the club, but these were their debuts after Schmeichel left.

MOST ENGLAND CAPS AS A UNITED PLAYER

	Player	England Career	Caps
1	Bobby Charlton	1958–70	106
2	Gary Neville	1995–2007	85
3	Bryan Robson	1981–91	77
4	Paul Scholes	1997–2004	66
5	David Beckham	1996–2003	60
6	Rio Ferdinand	2002–	53
6	Wayne Rooney	2004–	53
8	Phil Neville	1996–2005	52
9	Steve Coppell	1977–83	42
10	Ray Wilkins	1979–84	38

David Beckham is now the most-capped England outfield player of all time, with 115 in total. His first 60 caps came while he was at United. He made his England debut against Moldova in Chisinau on 1 September 1996 in a World Cup qualifier, but it was in the finals in France in 1998 that he had his low point, when he was sent off against Argentina. Roundly condemned by England fans, he set about redeeming himself, displaying brilliant form for United the next season on the way to the Treble. He was made England captain by caretaker manager Peter Taylor at the end of 2000, after Kevin Keegan resigned. He retained the position throughout Sven-Goran Eriksson's reign, and had arguably his finest hour in an England shirt when he gave an inspirational performance in the final World Cup qualifier against Greece to ensure England went to Japan and South Korea. Once there, his displays were constrained following a broken metatarsal, but he still managed to score against Argentina to knock them out of the tournament.

BIGGEST DEFEATS IN EUROPE

	Opposition	Venue	Date	Round	Score
1	Sporting Lisbon	Away	18 March 1964	ECWC QF	5–0
2	AC Milan	Away	14 May 1958	EC SF	4–0
2	Porto	Away	19 October 1977	ECWC 2nd	4–0
2	Barcelona	Away	2 November 1994	CL Gp	4–0
5	Juventus	Away	3 November 1976	UEFA 2nd	3–0
5	Atletico Madrid	Away	23 October 1991	ECWC 2nd	3–0
5	Maccabi Haifa	Away	29 October 2002	CL Gp 1	3–0
5	Fenerbahce	Away	8 December 2004	CL Gp	3–0
5	AC Milan	Away	2 May 2007	CL SF	3–0
10	Athletic Bilbao	Away	16 January 1957	EC QF	5–3

In 291 games in Europe, United have lost just 56 times and on only nine occasions has the margin been more than two goals. The worst result came in United's first campaign in the European Cup-Winners' Cup. Having reached the quarter-finals after victories over Willem II and trophy-holders Tottenham, United had comfortably beaten Sporting Lisbon 4–1 at Old Trafford. Denis Law had scored his second hat-trick of the tournament (including two penalties), and Bobby Charlton added the other goal. There could have been more goals for United, but it seemed enough on the club's return to European action for the first time since Munich. Yet within 12 minutes of the start of the second leg, the Portuguese side scored twice to put the tie in the balance. The whole side played poorly, and after the interval Lisbon took full advantage, scoring three more goals in quick succession. So United went out 6–4 on aggregate, and their humiliation was one of the rare occasions where Matt Busby lost his temper. As Pat Crerand admitted: 'We had deserved every word of his criticism.'

MOST APPEARANCES AS A SUBSTITUTE

	Player	Career	Appearances
1	Ole Gunnar Solskjaer	1996–2007	150
2	Ryan Giggs	1991–	129
3	Paul Scholes	1994–2011	124
4	John O'Shea	1999–2011	92
5	**Phil Neville**	**1995–2005**	**85**
6	Nicky Butt	1992–2004	80
7	Brian McClair	1987–98	73
8	Diego Forlan	2002–04	61
9	Darren Fletcher	2003–	59
10	David McCreery	1974–79	53

Phil Neville was part of the golden generation of young United players who came through the ranks in the early 1990s to go on to have exceptional careers at club and international level. But he nearly became a cricketer instead, having set a record at Lancashire 2nd XI to become the youngest player to score a century for them. However, football won through and he made his debut for the Reds at right-back on 28 January 1995, just three days after Eric Cantona's notorious kung-fu kick at Selhurst Park and a week after his 18th birthday, helping his side to a 5–2 win over Wrexham in the fourth round of the FA Cup. An adaptable player, he could play on either side of the defence or as a holding midfielder, and this flexibility often meant he lost out on a regular place in the team, despite being a highly valued member of the squad. In the summer of 2005, he was sold to Everton and soon became captain of the Merseyside club, making more than 260 appearances for the Toffees by the end of 2010–11.

MOST RECENT DENZIL HAROUN RESERVE
TEAM PLAYERS OF THE YEAR

	Player	Season	Apps (Goals)	Current Team
1	Oliver Gill	2010–11	0	Manchester United
2	Ritchie De Laet	2009–10	6	Manchester United[1]
3	James Chester	2008–09	1	Hull City
4	Richard Eckersley	2007–08	4	Burnley†
5	Kieran Lee	2006–07	3 (1)	Oldham Athletic
6	Giuseppe Rossi	2005–06	14 (4)	Villarreal
7	Sylvan Ebanks-Blake	2004–05	2 (1)	Wolverhampton W
8	David Jones	2003–04	4	Wolverhampton W★
9	Darren Fletcher	2002–03	292 (21)	Manchester United
10	John O'Shea	2001–02	393 (15)	Sunderland

Named after a former club director, this award honours the player who has most impressed during the season for the reserves. Oliver Gill is the latest recipient of this award, and if his face seems somewhat familiar, it is because he is the son of United chief executive David Gill. Just 20 years old, Gill is a tall central defender who will look to challenge the regular first-team defenders during 2011–12, having featured on the bench in the wins against Bolton Wanderers and West Ham without yet coming on to the pitch. He was part of the team that picked up the Manchester Senior Cup in May 2011, beating Bolton 3–1. He formed a reliable partnership at the heart of the defence with Scott Wootton and commented: 'I just want to keep progressing as I have done the last few years.' With the support of reserve-team boss Warren Joyce and the rest of the staff, there is every chance he will join the production line of young talent coming through the ranks at United.

★Became free agent at the end of 2010–11; †On loan to Toronto FC until January 2012; [1]On loan to Norwich City for 2011–12.

LEAGUE CUP FINALS

	Opponent	Date	Result	Scorers
1	Liverpool	26 March 1983	1–2	Whiteside
2	Sheffield Wednesday	21 April 1991	0–1	–
3	Nottingham Forest	12 April 1992	1–0	McClair
4	Aston Villa	27 March 1994	1–3	Hughes
5	Liverpool	2 March 2003	0–2	–
6	**Wigan Athletic**	**26 February 2006**	**4–0**	**Rooney 2, Ronaldo, Saha**
7	Tottenham Hotspur	1 March 2009	0–0	Won 4–1 on penalties
8	Aston Villa	28 February 2010	2–1	Owen, Rooney

Having lost four of the first five League Cup finals they reached, United have done much better in recent years, winning on the last three occasions. Only Liverpool have appeared in more finals than United's eight. The victory over Wigan was arguably the most significant of all of the Reds' successes in this tournament. Not only was the winning margin a record in the final, it showed the club was on its way back to the top. The previous season, United had failed to win any silverware, and in 2005–06 had not qualified for the knockout stages of the Champions League. Many outsiders were questioning if United could ever dominate again, as they had in the past, but Sir Alex knew how one trophy can lead to another. Gary Neville, who was picking up his first trophy as captain, commented afterwards: 'It is obvious to everybody that this club is growing.' While Ryan Giggs, with his own unmatched haul of medals, added: 'This is the first trophy for many of the players, so hopefully it can do what it did for me [in 1992] and give them a taste for success that makes you want more.' As the next three seasons brought five trophies, it certainly seemed to work.

MOST COMMON LEAGUE CUP OPPONENTS

	Opponent	Period	Times Met
1	Burnley	1969–2002	8
1	Tottenham Hotspur	1979–2009	8
3	**Aston Villa**	**1970–2010**	7
3	Middlesbrough	1969–2008	7
5	Arsenal	1977–2004	6
5	Manchester City	1969–2010	6
5	Oxford United	1972–1988	6
5	Port Vale	1983–1994	6
5	Portsmouth	1970–1994	6

United have met Aston Villa twice in the eight League Cup finals they have featured in during the club's history. The first occasion, in 1994, had an unhappy outcome as former manager Ron Atkinson celebrated beating United 3–1 and thus prevented the Reds from scooping a unique domestic treble. But on 28 February 2010 United emerged as the victors, retaining the trophy for the first time. The game was not without controversy. After just five minutes, Nemanja Vidic wrestled pacy Villa striker Gabriel Agbonlahor to the ground in the penalty area. The Serbian was penalised, but many felt he was fortunate not to see a red card as well – even Sir Alex called the decision a 'lucky break'. The spot kick converted, United soon hit back as Michael Owen latched on to Richard Dunne's attempted clearance. The Reds began to take charge, but it wasn't until the game was 74 minutes old that substitute Wayne Rooney (on for the injured Owen) was able to head home a cross from Antonio Valencia. For some it was their first trophy in United colours, but for Gary Neville it proved to be his last medal.

FIRST TEN MATCHES AT OLD TRAFFORD

	Opponents	Date	Score	Crowd	Scorers
1	Liverpool	19 February	3–4	45,000	A. Turnbull, Homer, Wall
2	Sheffield United	5 March	1–0	40,000	Picken
3	Bolton Wanderers	19 March	5–0	20,000	Halse, Meredith, Picken, J. Turnbull, Wall
4	Bristol City	25 March	2–1	50,000	Picken, J. Turnbull
5	Blackburn Rovers	2 April	2–0	20,000	Halse 2
6	Everton	6 April	3–2	5,500	J. Turnbull 2, Meredith
7	Sunderland	16 April	2–0	12,000	A. Turnbull, Wall
8	Middlesbrough	30 April	4–1	10,000	Picken 4
9	Blackburn Rovers	3 September	3–2	40,000	Meredith, A. Turnbull, West
10	Manchester City	17 September	2–1	60,000	A. Turnbull, West

When Manchester United moved into their new stadium in Trafford Park early in 1910, the club had the best ground in the country. With a capacity of up to 80,000, Old Trafford reflected the ambition of the chairman, John Henry Davies, and was designed by the famous architect Archibald Leitch. Davies had funded a trophy-winning side, but the old stadium at Bank Street was dilapidated, polluted and the pitch was often a quagmire, so he wanted a venue fit for champions. The first game at Old Trafford was played on a wet winter's day, in front of a good crowd – the official figures may have underestimated the numbers. Match-day receipts were £1,200, as fans paid between five shillings (25p) and sixpence (2½p) to get in. The first goal was scored by Sandy Turnbull with a low header. Though Tom Homer gave United a 2–0 lead, Liverpool came back to win 4–3. After that disappointment, United won their next nine games at Old Trafford, including the first Manchester derby played there, when Turnbull was again on target.

MOST APPEARANCES FOR UNITED BEFORE THE SECOND WORLD WAR

	Player	Career	Appearances
1	Joe Spence	1919–33	510
2	Jack Silcock	1919–34	449
3	Billy Meredith	1907–21	335
4	Charlie Moore	1919–30	328
5	Alfred Steward	1920–32	326
6	Clarence Hilditch	1919–32	322
7	George Wall	1906–15	319
8	Fred Erentz	1892–1902	310
9	Alex Bell	1903–13	309
10	Charlie Roberts	1904–13	302

Of all the great servants of Manchester United, Joe Spence has perhaps the lowest profile. The only pre-war player to feature in the Reds' all-time Top 10 appearance-makers, he played for United in their darkest era. He still lies fourth in the all-time list of league appearances, and is the sixth highest goalscorer for United. Born in 1898 in the mining village of Throckley, near Newcastle, he made his debut straight after the First World War where he had seen action as a machine gunner. A winger who often cut inside to score many goals, his best season came in 1927–28 when he found the net 24 times, including a hat-trick in the final game, against Liverpool at Old Trafford, that ensured United avoided relegation. Eventually he was sold to Bradford City in 1933. He made two appearances for England, earning his debut in a friendly against Belgium in May 1926 – the selectors having omitted to select him for the previous game, held at Old Trafford.

UNITED'S FIRST TEN
INTERNATIONAL PLAYERS★

	Player	Country	Debut	Apps (Goals)
1	Carlo Sartori	Italy	9 October 1968	55 (6)
2	Nikola Jovanovic	Yugoslavia	2 February 1980	26 (4)
3	Arnold Muhren	Netherlands	28 August 1982	98 (18)
4	Jesper Olsen	Denmark	25 August 1984	176 (24)
5	Johnny Sivebaek	Denmark	9 February 1986	34 (1)
6	Mark Bosnich	Australia	30 April 1990	38
7	Andrei Kanchelskis	Ukraine	11 May 1991	161 (36)
8	Peter Schmeichel	Denmark	17 August 1991	398 (1)
9	Eric Cantona	France	6 December 1992	185 (82)
10	William Prunier	France	30 December 1995	2

Although Arnold Muhren was a great success when he joined United, he was already well established in English football by then, after a spell at Ipswich Town, and at 31 was coming towards the end of his career. So Jesper Olsen was the first foreign signing to have a major impact at Old Trafford. He joined United from Ajax in the summer of 1984 for a fee of £350,000. A highly skilled winger, he usually worked on the left while fellow new signing Gordon Strachan patrolled the right. At 23, he had the potential to become an even better player, but a combination of injuries and a light physique meant that he did not consistently deliver as much as was hoped. In the end, he was sold to Bordeaux by Alex Ferguson in November 1988 for £400,000. His most prolific campaign came in 1985–86, when he scored 13 goals. He now lives and works in Australia, and sadly suffered a brain haemorrhage in 2006.

★List excludes those from Republic of Ireland, loan signings, as well as those of British families born abroad, such as Charlie Mitten or Jimmy Nicholl; also excluded are James Brown and Eddie McIlvenny, who both played for the USA in World Cups but were born in Britain.

PLAYERS WHO DON'T COME FROM WHERE YOU'D EXPECT

	Player	Career	Appearances	Goals
1	Alan Brazil	1984–86	41	12
2	Jim Cairns	1895–98	2	0
3	James Chester	2008	1	0
4	Dion Dublin	1992–94	17	3
5	Stewart Houston	1974–80	250	16
6	Joe Jordan	1978–81	126	41
7	Joe Lancaster	1950–51	4	0
8	Stephen Preston	1901–03	34	14
9	Harry Stafford	1896–1903	200	1
10	**Antonio Valencia**	2009–	69	10

Antonio Valencia is not from the east coast of Spain, but comes from Ecuador. He was born on 4 August 1985 in Nueva Loja, close to the Colombian border. The town has a population of some 25,000 but was founded only some 20 years earlier when the first oil well started operation in March 1967. He began his career at El Nacional, one of the most successful clubs in the country, based in the capital Quito, before moving to Villarreal in 2005. He struggled to win a place in the side, and was eventually signed by Wigan, initially on loan, after impressing during the 2006 World Cup. When Cristiano Ronaldo left United, Valencia was the man signed up to replace him. Undaunted by that challenge, he set about establishing himself in the Reds team, playing to his strengths – pace, physical presence and an ability to supply superb crosses – rather than trying to be another Ronaldo. His progress was temporarily halted by a horrendous injury early in 2010–11, but he came back near the end of the season in fine form.

THEY PLAYED FOR UNITED AND CITY*

	Player	United Career (Apps, Goals)	City Career
1	Denis Law	1962–73 (404, 237)	1959–61, 1973–74
2	Brian Kidd	1967–74 (266, 70)	1976–79
3	Sammy McIlroy	1971–82 (419, 71)	1985–86
4	Wyn Davies	1972–73 (17, 4)	1971–72
5	John Gidman	1981–86 (120, 4)	1986–88
6	Peter Beardsley	1982 (1)	1998
7	Peter Barnes	1985–86 (25, 4)	1974–79, 1987
8	Mark Robins	1988–92 (70, 17)	1999
9	Andrei Kanchelskis	1991–95 (161, 36)	2001
10	Peter Schmeichel	1991–99 (398, 1)	2002–03
11	Carlos Tevez	2007–09 (99, 34)	2009–

Of all the players to have turned out for both Manchester clubs, none has had such a significant role to play with both sides as Brian Kidd. A local lad from Collyhurst, Kidd made his debut for United in a famous Charity Shield match at Old Trafford in August 1967, when he set up Bobby Charlton for one of his greatest-ever goals. By the end of the campaign, he was in action at Wembley in the European Cup final against Benfica, when he scored one goal and laid on the final pass for two more, as United emerged 4–1 winners. Not a bad way to celebrate your 19th birthday! It surprised many when he moved to Arsenal for a fee of £110,000 in 1974, but two years later he was back in Manchester – this time playing at Maine Road, when he had the most prolific period of his career. However, that wasn't the end of the story; after he retired as a player, he had spells at both clubs as assistant manager to Alex Ferguson and Roberto Mancini, respectively.

*Since the Second World War.

SCOTTISH OPPONENTS IN
EUROPEAN COMPETITIONS

	Opponents	Venue	Date	Competition	Score
1	Dundee United	Home	28 November 1984	UEFA 3rd	2–2
2	Dundee United	Away	12 December 1984	UEFA 3rd	3–2
3	**Rangers**	**Away**	**22 October 2003**	**CL Group**	**1–0**
4	Rangers	Home	4 November 2003	CL Group	3–0
5	Celtic	Home	13 September 2006	CL Group	3–2
6	Celtic	Away	21 November 2006	CL Group	0–1
7	Celtic	Home	21 October 2008	CL Group	3–0
8	Celtic	Away	5 November 2008	CL Group	1–1
9	Rangers	Home	14 September 2010	CL Group	0–0
10	Rangers	Away	24 November 2010	CL Group	1–0

Throughout United's history there have been just ten official matches against teams from Scotland. United's first game at Ibrox against Rangers was particularly significant, as this saw Sir Alex Ferguson return to his former club. He played for Rangers for two years between 1967 and 1969, and had grown up within a mile of the stadium, having supported the club as a boy, but his spell there had ended in disappointment. It wasn't Sir Alex's only link with the past, for the Rangers manager that day was Alex McLeish, who had played for him when he was manager of Aberdeen. Somewhat surprisingly, the winning goal was scored by Phil Neville, one of just eight he scored in 386 appearances for United. That day, he was preferred to Cristiano Ronaldo on the wide right, and linked up with Ruud van Nistelrooy to score a superb winner after just five minutes. In this Anglo–Scottish battle, no Scots played for either side, but United had four Englishmen in their starting line-up (Gary and Phil Neville, Rio Ferdinand and Paul Scholes).

MOST LEAGUE GOALS IN A SEASON

	Player	Season	Appearances (Sub)	Goals
1	Dennis Viollet	1959–60	36	32
2	Cristiano Ronaldo	2007–08	31 (3)	31
3	Jack Rowley	1951–52	40	30
3	Denis Law	1963–64	30	30
5	Bobby Charlton	1958–59	38	29
6	Denis Law	1964–65	36	28
6	George Best	1967–68	41	28
8	Jack Rowley	1946–47	37	26
8	Wayne Rooney	2009–10	32	26
10	Sandy Turnbull	1907–08	30	25
10	Tommy Taylor	1955–56	33	25
10	Ruud van Nistelrooy	2002–03	33 (1)	25

In the modern game, it is exceptionally rare for a striker to score 30-plus goals in a league season – for a winger to do it is unheard of. And yet that was what Cristiano Ronaldo achieved in what was surely his best campaign for the Reds. The Portugal international from the island of Madeira had impressed United when he had played against them for Sporting Lisbon, and Sir Alex Ferguson moved quickly to snap him up. He was just 18 when he made his United debut in August 2003, and as he matured he grew into one of the most dazzling talents ever to pull on the United jersey. In 2007–08, he seemed unstoppable, and it was fitting he should score the final goal of the league campaign, which United ended as champions, two points clear of Chelsea. He scored his only hat-trick for United against Newcastle United that season, too.

BIGGEST WINS AGAINST MANCHESTER CITY

	Date	Venue	Score	Scorers
1	10 November 1994	Old Trafford	5–0	Cantona, Kanchelskis 3, Hughes
2	3 October 1891	North Road	5–1	Farman 2, R. Doughty, Edge, Sneddon
2	31 December 1960	Old Trafford	5–1	Dawson 3, Charlton 2
4	3 November 1894	Hyde Road	5–2	Smith 4, Clarkin
5	31 August 1957	Old Trafford	4–1	Berry, Edwards, T. Taylor, Viollet
5	16 February 1959	Old Trafford	4–1	Bradley 2, Goodwin, Scanlon
5	5 January 1895	Bank Street	4–1	Clarkin 2, Donaldson, Smith
8	10 September 1898	Bank Street	3–0	Boyd, Cassidy, Collinson
8	24 January 1970	Old Trafford	3–0	Kidd 2, Morgan
8	10 February 1979	Maine Road	3–0	Coppell 2, Ritchie
8	14 September 1985	Maine Road	3–0	Albiston, Duxbury, Robson
8	11 February 1995	Maine Road	3–0	Cole, Ince, Kanchelskis

For United's fans there is nothing quite to rival the battle to become the top team in Manchester. United got off to a great start, in their days as Newton Heath, as their first three fixtures against City all feature in the list above. But the biggest win remains the 5–0 thrashing in the 1994–95 season. That campaign, Ukrainian winger Andrei Kanchelskis finished up as the club's leading scorer. He scored his only hat-trick for the Reds in this match, which many fans saw as long-awaited revenge for a 5–1 defeat the club had suffered five years before. His link-up play with Eric Cantona, combined with his raw pace, meant he was unstoppable. He scored either side of half-time, and completed his hat-trick late in the game. Kanchelskis went on to score hat-tricks in the Liverpool and Glasgow derbies, for Everton and Rangers – the only man to have achieved the feat in all three cities.

MOST APPEARANCES FOR
RON ATKINSON'S SIGNINGS

	Player	Career	Appearances	Goals
1	Bryan Robson	1981–94	461	99
2	Frank Stapleton	1981–87	288	78
3	Gordon Strachan	1984–89	201	38
4	Paul McGrath	1982–89	199	16
4	Remi Moses	1981–88	199	12
6	Jesper Olsen	1984–88	176	24
7	John Gidman	1981–86	120	4
8	Peter Davenport	1986–88	106	26
9	Arnold Muhren	1982–85	98	18
10	Colin Gibson	1985–90	95	9

During Ron Atkinson's reign, from 1981 to 1986, there is one signing that stands out head and shoulders above everyone else: Bryan Robson. Brought in from Atkinson's former club West Brom for a record fee of £1.5 million, Robson was already established in the centre of midfield for England and, at 24, had his best years ahead of him. He became the ultimate 'Captain Marvel' for club and country, never more so than when he inspired the Reds to a stunning comeback in the 1984 European Cup-Winners' Cup tie against Barcelona, taking on Maradona and all. He led from the front on the pitch, in training and even when it came to team-bonding away from the pitch. So vital did he become to United's fortunes, his absence from the line-up would often result in the team losing. In all, he won six trophies for United, before leaving for Middlesbrough in 1994 to become their player-manager. Incredibly, he never won either the FWA or PFA player of the year awards.

MOST HAT-TRICKS IN A SEASON

	Player	Season	Hat-tricks
1	Denis Law	1963–64	7
2	Jack Rowley	1951–52	4
2	Denis Law	1968–69	4
4	Joe Cassidy	1896–97	3
4	Henry Boyd	1897–98	3
4	Jack Picken	1905–06	3
4	Alex 'Sandy' Turnbull	1907–08	3
4	Jack Rowley	1947–48	3
4	Denis Law	1962–63	3
4	David Herd	1965–66	3
4	Ruud van Nistelrooy	2002–03	3
4	**Dimitar Berbatov**	**2010–11**	3

In 2010–11, United's record signing Dimitar Berbatov became only the second man in the last 40 years to score a hat-trick of hat-tricks in a season for the Reds. Just eight players had previously managed this feat for United, with Denis Law doing it three times and Jack Rowley twice. It was the Bulgarian's most prolific season of his career in England. His first hat-trick was especially popular, coming in September against Liverpool. After scoring from a Giggs corner, he put United 2–0 up with a brilliant bicycle kick. Liverpool fought back to 2–2, before Berbatov clinched all three points with a great header from a John O'Shea cross. In November, he hit five against Blackburn Rovers, as the Reds went on the rampage, winning 7–1. Then in January it was the turn of Birmingham to feel the full force of the elegant and enigmatic striker, as he hit three in United's 5–0 romp.

FORMER UNITED PLAYERS AS MANAGERS
IN 2010–11

	Player	Club(s) Managed	United Career
1	Sammy McIlroy	Morecambe	1971–82
2	Steve Coppell	Bristol City	1975–83
3	Mark Hughes	Fulham	1983–95
4	Gordon Strachan	Middlesbrough	1984–89
5	Chris Turner	Hartlepool United	1985–88
6	Steve Bruce	Sunderland	1987–96
7	Mark Robins	Barnsley	1988–92
8	**Paul Ince**	**Notts County**	**1989–95**
9	Darren Ferguson	Preston North End/Peterborough United	1991–93
10	Roy Keane	Ipswich Town	1993–2005

The 2010–11 campaign was not a great season for former United players in their managerial roles, with only Steve Bruce remaining in position all the way to the end of May. However, Darren Ferguson bounced back from his departure at Preston to lead Peterborough to promotion. Paul Ince has been a trailblazer in many ways, as he became the first black player to captain England while at United and then the first black Englishman to manage in the top level of English football, having a brief period in charge of Blackburn Rovers in 2008. Signed by Alex Ferguson from West Ham in 1989, he was part of the Scot's first great side at United that won numerous trophies between 1990 and 1994, including United's first Premier League title in 1992–93. That season, United's side featured four of the above – Bruce, Ferguson, Hughes, Ince – plus Bryan Robson, all of whom became managers, while Brian McClair and Mike Phelan went on to coaching roles at United. After the 1994–95 season, Ince was sold to Inter Milan to make way for Nicky Butt.

UNITED OLD BOYS AT OLD TRAFFORD
IN 2010–11

	Player	Team	Date	Result
1	Alan Smith	Newcastle United	16 August 2010	3–0
2	Jonathan Spector	West Ham United	28 August 2010	3–0
3	Sylvan Ebanks-Blake	Wolverhampton W	6 November 2010	2–1 (g)
4	Phil Bardsley	Sunderland	26 December 2010	2–0
5	Ryan Shawcross	Stoke City	4 January 2011	2–1
6	Ben Foster	Birmingham City	22 January 2011	5–0
7	Carlos Tevez	Manchester City	12 February 2011	2–1
8	Jonathan Greening	Fulham	9 April 2011	2–0
9	**Tim Howard**	**Everton**	**23 April 2011**	**1–0**
10	Phil Neville	Everton	23 April 2011	1–0

All the ex-United players who came back to Old Trafford in the 2010–11 season tasted defeat, with just former Denzil Haroun Reserve Team Player of the Year Sylvan Ebanks-Blake having any joy, scoring a close-range equaliser. But it was the Everton pair of Tim Howard and Phil Neville who had the longest United careers. For Howard, it was yet another defeat on his homecoming. The American goalkeeper had joined the Reds in the summer of 2003 from MetroStars, the MLS side based in his home state of New Jersey. By that stage, he had already won his first cap for the US (a hotly contested position, given the competition from Brad Friedel, Kasey Keller and Marcus Hahnemann) and has now won more than 60. After a bright start, he made one or two costly errors but still became the first American to win an FA Cup medal, in 2004. In 2006, he moved to Everton, and since joining the Merseyside outfit he has set a club record for clean sheets in a season, in 2008–09.

THE BUSBY BABES

	Player	Debut	Opposition	Age
1	David Gaskell	24 October 1956	Manchester City	16y 19d
2	Jeff Whitefoot	15 April 1950	Portsmouth	16y 105d
3	**Duncan Edwards**	**4 April 1953**	**Cardiff City**	**16y 185d**
4	Alex Dawson	22 April 1957	Birmingham City	17y 60d
5	David Pegg	6 December 1952	Middlesbrough	17y 77d
6	Cliff Birkett	2 December 1950	Newcastle United	17y 80d
7	Mark Jones	7 October 1950	Sheffield Wednesday	17y 114d
8	John Doherty	6 December 1952	Middlesbrough	17y 269d
9	Brian Birch	27 August 1949	West Bromwich A	17y 282d
10	Eddie Lewis	29 November 1952	West Bromwich A	17y 330d
11	Wilf McGuinness	8 October 1955	Wolverhampton W	17y 348d

The list above includes all those players aged under 18 who made their debuts for Matt Busby's United prior to Munich. It is an extraordinary roll-call of talent, and shows the faith the manager placed in the youngsters the club developed through its ranks. But one man stands clear above the rest: Duncan Edwards. He was a phenomenon: he had a shot so hard it could burst a ball or knock out a goalkeeper, a sublime range of passing, was unstoppable in the tackle and powerful in the air, could dribble superbly, and ran all day for the team. The only problem Busby had was to decide his best position, as he could play anywhere. He was just 21 when he lost his life at Munich, but was already the winner of two league titles and an England regular, tipped as a future captain. As Busby said: 'If there was ever a player who could be called a one-man team, that man was Duncan Edwards.'

HIGHEST ATTENDANCES FOR UNITED MATCHES*

	Opposition	Venue	Date	Competition	Score	Crowd
1	Real Madrid	Bernabeu	11 Apr 1957	EC SF	1–3	135,000
2	Real Madrid	Bernabeu	15 May 1968	EC SF	3–3	125,000
3	Barcelona	Nou Camp	2 Nov 1994	CL Gp	0–4	114,273
4	Gornik Zabrze	Slaski[1]	13 Mar 1968	EC QF	0–1	105,000
5	Barcelona	Nou Camp	23 Apr 2008	CL SF	0–0	95,949
6	Bradford PA	Maine Road†	29 Jan 1949	FA Cup 4th	1–1	82,771
7	Arsenal	Maine Road†	17 Jan 1948	Div 1	1–1	81,962
8	Yeovil Town	Maine Road†	12 Feb 1949	FA Cup 5th	8–0	81,565
9	Inter Milan	San Siro	24 Feb 2009	CL 2nd	0–0	80,018
10	AC Milan	San Siro	14 May 1958	EC SF	0–4	80,000
10	AC Milan	San Siro	23 Apr 1969	EC SF	0–2	80,000
10	AC Milan	San Siro	16 Feb 2010	CL 2nd	3–2	80,000

The two biggest crowds United have ever played in front of were both in Madrid. The first occasion ended in disappointment, but the second took the Reds through to an emotional European Cup final at Wembley. Having taken a slender 1–0 lead from the first leg, United knew they would have a tough challenge in front of a passionate Spanish crowd. After little more than 30 minutes the Reds were 2–0 down, before both sides scored just ahead of half time to make it 3–2 on aggregate. Although United had been outplayed, they were still very much in the tie, as Matt Busby reminded them in the break. David Sadler, who had been playing in a holding role, took a more positive approach and got his reward when he hit home from a George Best header. Best then created a third goal, five minutes later, with Bill Foulkes the surprise scorer.

*Excluding cup finals; †United's home ground while Old Trafford was being repaired after the war; [1]some sources quote the attendance as 77,649.

TOP 10 MANAGERS IN NOVEMBER 1986

	Manager	Club	Date left
1	Brian Clough	Nottingham Forest	8 May 1993
2	George Graham	Arsenal	21 February 1995
3	Kenny Dalglish	Liverpool	22 February 1991
4	John Lyall	West Ham United	5 June 1989
5	Ken Brown	Norwich City	9 November 1987
6	Howard Kendall	Everton	18 June 1987
7	John Moore	Luton Town	15 June 1987
8	George Curtis	Coventry City	2 June 1987
9	David Pleat	Tottenham Hotspur	23 October 1987
10	Dave Bassett	Wimbledon	11 May 1987

When Alex Ferguson arrived at Manchester United on 6 November 1986, the club was lying in 19th place but finished the campaign in a comfortable 11th position. This list shows the managers of the top ten clubs that the new man was up against on the day he joined; amazingly, only four were still in place just over a year later. Four of Ferguson's original rivals have a league title on their CV (Clough, Dalglish, Graham and Kendall), but only George Graham has a direct link with United. The Scottish international midfielder was signed by Tommy Docherty from Arsenal for a hefty fee of £120,000 and made his debut against his former club on 6 January 1973, but was moved on in November 1974. However, Graham had more success as a manager and is the only former United player ever to manage a championship-winning side; at Arsenal he won the League Cup in 1987, the league in 1989 and 1991, the League Cup and FA Cup in 1993, and the European Cup-Winners' Cup in 1994. At Spurs he won the League Cup again in 1999.

TEAM FOR ALEX FERGUSON'S
FIRST TROPHY

	Player	Career	Appearances	Goals
1	Les Sealey	1990–94	56	0
2	Paul Ince	1989–95	281	29
3	Lee Martin	1988–93	109	2
4	Steve Bruce	1987–96	414	51
5	Mike Phelan	1989–93	146	3
6	Gary Pallister	1989–98	437	15
7	Bryan Robson	1981–94	461	99
8	Neil Webb	1989–92	110	11
9	Brian McClair	1987–98	471	127
10	Mark Hughes	1983–95	467	163
11	Danny Wallace	1989–93	71	11

After joining United in November 1986, Alex Ferguson was still looking for his first trophy at the club when he got his chance in the 1990 FA Cup final, when the Reds took on Crystal Palace. Although both sides had finished in the bottom half of the table, United were favourites, but ended up drawing 3–3 with the Eagles, meaning a replay was required. Lee Martin scored the only goal of the second game, but most attention centred on the selection of Les Sealey, who had replaced regular keeper Jim Leighton after the first encounter. Going with the eccentric but experienced Sealey was a brave move, and a controversial one, but it showed that the manager would always take what he saw as the right decision for the club, rather than relying on sentiment. Sealey performed superbly, and donated his medal to Leighton afterwards. Given his short career, it is surprising to note that he appeared in three other finals in his 56 appearances.

THE WORLD'S MOST VALUABLE FOOTBALL TEAMS*

	Team	Country	Value ($m)
1	Manchester United	England	1,830
2	Real Madrid	Spain	1,320
3	Arsenal	England	1,180
4	Barcelona	Spain	1,000
5	Bayern Munich	Germany	990
6	Liverpool	England	822
7	AC Milan	Italy	800
8	Juventus	Italy	656
9	Chelsea	England	646

United dominate this list to an extraordinary extent, yet the story was very different 30 years ago. In 1984 the *Daily Mirror* reported that the paper's owner, Robert Maxwell, was planning a takeover bid valuing the club at £10 million. Five years later, in autumn 1989, Michael Knighton displayed his trickery in front of a disbelieving Stretford End, but his offer of £20 million for the club eventually fell through. By the end of the year, then chairman Martin Edwards said he would accept a bid of £30 million. When the club became a PLC in 1991, the club was worth £47 million. If that rate of increase in the value of United was spectacular, the Premier League accelerated things. With the stadium expanding and interest in football seemingly at a peak, in 1998 Rupert Murdoch offered £575 million for United, later increased to £625 million, but the government stopped the deal going through. When the Glazer family bought United in 2005, they had to pay around £800 million for the biggest club in the world, but according to *Forbes*, the value has gone up yet again.

*According to *Forbes* 'The 50 Most Valuable Teams in Sports', 21 July 2010.

THE WORLD'S MOST VALUABLE
SPORTS TEAMS★

	Team	Sport	Value ($m)
1	Manchester United	Football	1,830
2	Dallas Cowboys	American Football	1,650
3	New York Yankees	Baseball	1,600
4	Washington Redskins	American Football	1,550
5	New England Patriots	American Football	1,360
6	Real Madrid	Football	1,320
7	New York Giants	American Football	1,180
7	Arsenal	Football	1,180
9	New York Jets	American Football	1,170
10	Houston Texans	American Football	1,150

According to the research carried out by *Forbes*, all but 11 of the 50 most valuable sports teams in the world are based in America. The exceptions are nine football teams (see previous entry) and two Formula One teams (Ferrari and McLaren). In such a list, where the emphasis is on the other side of the Atlantic, it is all the more impressive that United comes out on top – and comfortably so. *Forbes* quoted United's core worldwide fanbase as being 139 million, with more than 330 million other followers globally – no wonder the Reds are out on their own. In making their calculations, *Forbes* looked at United's link-up with Nike, quoted as being worth $470 million over 13 years, plus a 50 per cent share of the profits on specific merchandise. Then there was the shirt sponsorship deal with Aon, which they valued at $34 million per year. Add in TV revenue, matchday receipts and much else besides and you begin to see why United is truly the greatest sports club in the world.

★According to *Forbes* 'The 50 Most Valuable Teams in Sports', 21 July 2010.

MOST CONSECUTIVE LEAGUE APPEARANCES

	Player	Start	Finish	Apps
1	Steve Coppell	19 January 1977	7 November 1981	206
2	Allenby Chilton	10 March 1951	23 February 1955	166
3	Martin Buchan	4 March 1972	5 April 1975	136
4	Arthur Albiston	12 March 1980	23 April 1983	132
5	Brian McClair	15 August 1987	21 April 1990	113
6	Charlie Mitten	6 March 1948	29 April 1950	97
7	Steve Bruce	14 March 1992	1 May 1994	94
7	Peter Schmeichel	14 March 1992	1 May 1994	94
9	Sammy McIlroy	23 March 1974	21 April 1976	92
10	Joe Cassidy	27 March 1897	17 February 1900	90
10	Denis Irwin	21 November 1992	28 December 1994	90

Allenby Chilton was the first United player in history to appear in more than 100 consecutive league games. He came from the mining area of County Durham and was as tough as a pit prop. He actually joined United before the war, and played at the start of the 1939–40 season, but those games were expunged from the record books when war broke out, so his 'official' debut did not come until January 1946 in the FA Cup. During the war, he had fought in Normandy, and been injured in combat, so as a robust centre-half he feared nothing his opponents could throw at him. He was part of the 1948 FA Cup-winning side, and his unbroken run in the side coincided with United's league title triumph in 1951–52. By 1953–54, he was club captain, but eventually lost his place to Mark Jones (after making 391 appearances in total, scoring just three goals) and so moved on to become player-manager at Grimsby.

UNITED'S MOST LEAGUE GOALS IN A SEASON

	Season	Division	Position	Games	Goals
1	1956–57	Div 1	1st	42	103
1	1958–59	Div 1	2nd	42	103
3	1959–60	Div 1	7th	42	102
4	1999–2000	PL	1st	38	97
5	1946–47	Div 1	2nd	42	95
5	1951–52	Div 1	1st	42	95
7	1905–06	Div 2	2nd	38	90
7	1963–64	Div 1	2nd	42	90
9	1964–65	Div 1	1st	42	89
9	1967–68	Div 1	2nd	42	89

There are many reasons, of course, why the Busby Babes hold such a special place in the hearts of all United fans, but before the tragedy came the astonishing success of Busby's youthful side. In 1955–56 they won the league by a vast 11 points, but the following year they were determined to improve on that and played a compelling, irresistible brand of attacking football. As centre-forward that season, United had Tommy Taylor, who was the most prolific goalscorer in the club's history. At inside-forward was Dennis Viollet, who holds the club record for the most league goals in a season. Playing either on the wing or at inside-forward was United's all-time record goalscorer Bobby Charlton. And yet they were all outgunned by inside-forward Billy Whelan, who hit 26 that season, including a run of eight goals in consecutive matches. The quiet young Dubliner may not have had much pace, but he had great control and an eye for goal. Who knows what he would have gone on to achieve had he survived Munich.

PFA PLAYERS OF THE YEAR

	Player	Season
1	Mark Hughes	1988–89
2	Mark Hughes	1990–91
3	Gary Pallister	1991–92
4	Eric Cantona	1993–94
5	**Roy Keane**	**1999–2000**
6	Teddy Sheringham	2000–01
7	Ruud van Nistelrooy	2001–02
8	Cristiano Ronaldo	2006–07
9	Cristiano Ronaldo	2007–08
10	Ryan Giggs	2008–09
11	Wayne Rooney	2009–10

Since 1973–74, the members of the Professional Footballers' Association have voted for who they believe to have been the best player each season. Roy Keane, the driving force of United's title-winning side, deservedly took the award in 1999–2000. The Irishman joined the Reds from Nottingham Forest in the summer of 1993, signing for a record fee of £3.75 million. He had his share of injury problems, but when he took over the captaincy in the late 1990s he became the personification of United's never-say-die attitude, inspiring all around him and always looking to take on the next challenge. At his peak, he seemed an unstoppable force of nature. For many, his greatest game was in the Champions League semi-final against Juventus in 1999, when he led the side to a famous win in Italy. He left United in 2005 after 480 appearances, having scored 51 goals. In any debate about the club's greatest midfielders, Keane is one name always sure to figure.

MOST FA CUP FINALS

	Team	Last Appearance	Total
1	Manchester United	2007	18
2	Arsenal	2005	17
3	Everton	2009	13
3	Liverpool	2006	13
3	Newcastle United	1999	13
6	Aston Villa	2000	10
6	Chelsea	2010	10
6	West Bromwich Albion	1968	10
9	Manchester City	2011	9
9	Tottenham Hotspur	1991	9

Manchester United hold the record for the most appearances in the FA Cup final: 18 between 1909 and 2007. Of all the occasions the club has got to the showpiece finale, the one where United was without doubt the neutrals' favourite came in 1958, in the aftermath of the Munich disaster. The club had already reached the fifth round, after victories over Workington and Ipswich Town, by the time tragedy struck. Their first game afterwards was in the FA Cup, when on a hugely emotional night at Old Trafford, United beat Sheffield Wednesday 3–0. It took a replay to beat West Brom in the sixth round, and another to overcome Second Division Fulham in the semi-final. In the final, United met Bolton Wanderers, while Matt Busby made his first appearance on the touchline since recovering from his injuries in the crash. Sadly, there was to be no happy ending, as the Trotters won 2–0, taking an early lead through Nat Lofthouse. He then bundled ball and goalkeeper into the goal for a controversial second score soon after half-time.

PROGRESSION OF RECORD HOLDERS
FOR MOST GOALS

	Player	Career	Gained Record	Goals
1	Bob Donaldson*	1892–97	27 January 1894	66
2	Joe Cassidy	1893–1900	17 September 1898	100
3	George Wall†	1906–15	24 October 1914	100
4	Alex 'Sandy' Turnbull	1907–15	10 April 1915	101
5	Joe Spence[1]	1919–33	22 October 1927	168
6	Jack Rowley	1937–55	8 March 1952	211
7	Bobby Charlton	1956–73	22 November 1969	249

In United's first golden era under the management of Ernest Mangnall, inside-forward Sandy Turnbull was a vital figure. Born in Kilmarnock in 1884, the Scot joined the Reds from Manchester City and made his United debut on 1 January 1907 after his former club had been caught making illegal payments and were forced to sell many of their stars. He was the leading scorer in the championship-winning side of 1907–08, with 27 (his best total), scored the winner in the 1909 FA Cup final, and went on to score the first goal at Old Trafford. His final goal came on 10 April 1915, against Middlesbrough, to help earn a 2–2 draw and prevent relegation. However, there had been controversy eight days earlier (and four matches before – a hectic Easter schedule had intervened) when United had beaten Liverpool 2–0 at Old Trafford. Turnbull wasn't playing, but he was accused of match-fixing and banned from football, as local bookmakers had taken an unusual number of bets on the match finishing with that score. He always denied the allegations, but then lost his life in the fighting at Arras on 3 May 1917 and was subsequently granted a posthumous pardon.

*First to reach 20 goals; †Wall equalled the record on this date; [1]broke record by scoring a hat-trick.

MOST GOALS IN A UNITED CAREER

	Player	Career	Appearances	Goals
1	Bobby Charlton	1956–73	758	249
2	Denis Law	1963–73	404	237
3	Jack Rowley	1937–55	424	211
4	Dennis Viollet	1953–61	293	179
4	George Best	1963–74	470	179
6	Joe Spence	1919–33	510	168
7	Mark Hughes	1983–95	467	163
8	Ryan Giggs	1991–	876	159
9	Ruud van Nistelrooy	2001–06	219	150
9	Paul Scholes	1994–2011	676	150

Bobby Charlton has lost many of his club records to Ryan Giggs. But one that should be safe for a while yet is the all-time goalscoring record. For someone who played the bulk of his career in the midfield or on the wing, it is an astonishing achievement to have scored so many goals (he is also England's leading goalscorer). Part of the golden generation of the Busby Babes, Charlton was signed as a professional by United in 1954 and eventually made his debut on 6 October 1956, appropriately enough against Charlton Athletic, five days before his 19th birthday. United were heading for a second successive title, and Charlton scored twice on that occasion, in the 32nd and 37th minute, with two thumping shots that would become his trademark. His most prolific season was in 1958–59 when he hit an impressive 29 goals, including one of his seven career hat-tricks. His last goal came on 31 March 1973 in a 2–0 win against Southampton, and for the third time in his career he ended the season as United's leading scorer.

UNITED'S MOST COMMON OPPONENTS

	Opponent	Played	Won	Drawn	Lost	Percentage Wins*
1	Arsenal	212	88	46	78	41.51
2	Everton	182	79	41	62	43.41
2	Liverpool	182	71	50	61	39.01
4	Aston Villa	176	89	38	49	50.57
5	Tottenham Hotspur	174	82	46	46	47.13
6	Chelsea	161	70	47	44	43.48
7	Manchester City	159	66	50	43	41.51
8	Newcastle United	152	77	36	39	50.66
9	Sunderland	131	56	36	39	42.75
10	Sheffield Wednesday	124	54	27	43	43.55

Not one of United's most familiar opponents has a positive record against the Reds, Arsenal coming the closest. The two sides first met way back on 13 October 1894 in the Second Division, when Newton Heath (as United were then known) drew 3–3 with Arsenal at Bank Street. They have been frequent opponents in cup finals and semi-finals, though they had to wait until 1979 for their first meeting at this stage, when Arsenal won the FA Cup 3–2 after a dramatic climax to an otherwise dull game. In 1983, United got their revenge, winning the semi-finals of both the League Cup and FA Cup. United won the FA Cup semi-final in 1999, a game clinched by Ryan Giggs' famous solo effort. In 2004, it was another semi-final victory for United, reversed on a penalty shootout the following season in the final. Then, in 2009, United comprehensively outplayed Arsenal to go through to the final of the Champions League. So United remain undefeated in semi-finals against Arsenal, while Arsenal have beaten United in every final they've contested.

*Matches decided on penalty kicks are denoted here as drawn.

MOST TROPHIES WON OVERALL★

	Team	League	FA Cup	League Cup	Europe	Total
1	Liverpool	18	7	7	7	39
2	Manchester United	19	11	4	4	38
3	Arsenal	13	10	2	2	27
4	Aston Villa	7	7	5	1	20
5	Tottenham Hotspur	2	8	4	3	17
6	Chelsea	4	6	4	1	15
6	Everton	9	5	0	1	15
8	Newcastle United	4	6	0	1	11
9	Blackburn Rovers	3	6	1	0	10
9	Manchester City	2	5	2	1	10

While United may have overtaken Liverpool in the number of league titles won, the club remains one behind their Merseyside rivals in the overall total of major trophies gained. The last time the two sides went head-to-head with each other for a trophy was in 2008-09 when Liverpool were runners-up to United in the Premier League title race. After winning both the Premier League and the Champions League the previous season, United were slow to get started, taking just four points from four games, as Chelsea set the pace, followed by Liverpool. By December, the Anfield outfit was top, but after Christmas United won 11 successive games to go top, while Rafa had his famous rant. Liverpool could even come to Old Trafford and win 4-1 (United's biggest home defeat since 1992) and still not catch up, as both sides dropped just two points in their last nine games. It was an Old Trafford 0-0 draw against Arsenal in the penultimate fixture that was enough to see United confirm their 18th league title.

★European trophies do not include one-offs such as the Super Cup.

THE MUNICH AIR DISASTER

Player	Debut	Age	Apps	Goals
Geoff Bent	11 December 1954	25	12	0
Roger Byrne	**24 November 1951**	**28**	**280**	**20**
Eddie Colman	12 November 1955	21	108	2
Duncan Edwards	4 April 1953	21	177	21
Mark Jones	7 October 1950	24	121	1
David Pegg	6 December 1952	22	150	28
Tommy Taylor	7 March 1953	26	191	131
Billy Whelan	26 March 1955	22	98	52
Walter Crickmer (Club Secretary)		58	n/a	n/a
Tom Curry (trainer)		63	n/a	n/a
Bert Whalley (coach)	30 November 1935	45	38	0

There were 43 people on the aeroplane that crashed on the runway at Munich airport on 6 February 1958. Twenty-three people died in the disaster, among them eight players and three of the backroom staff at Manchester United. It was a tragedy that resonated around the world, for this was a team whose fame was increasing and whose exciting skills delighted so many – and suddenly they were gone. Roger Byrne was the oldest and most experienced player of the Busby Babes who lost their lives, and had succeeded Johnny Carey as captain of the side. He was the only player in the side who had been a part of United's 1951–52 title-winning campaign. A speedy left-back, his pace meant he was occasionally drafted in to play left-wing, and once he made his debut he rarely missed a game in the six years that followed. For England, too, he was a regular pick, selected for 33 successive games from his debut in April 1954.

LONGEST-SERVING MANAGERS

	Manager	Joined	Left	Total
1	Sir Alex Ferguson	November 1986	–	24 years 9 months
2	Sir Matt Busby	October 1945	June 1971★	24 years 1 month
3	**Walter Crickmer**	**April 1931**	**October 1945†**	**9 years 4 months**
4	Ernest Mangnall	September 1903	August 1912	8 years 11 months
5	John Robson	August 1914	October 1921	7 years 2 months
6	Ron Atkinson	May 1981	November 1986	5 years 6 months
7	Scott Duncan	August 1932	October 1937	5 years 2 months
8	John Chapman	October 1921	September 1926	4 years 11 months
9	Tommy Docherty	December 1972	July 1977	4 years 7 months
10	Herbert Bamlett	May 1927	April 1931	3 years 11 months

Although he was manager for just 119 competitive matches, Walter Crickmer was the third longest-serving boss in United's history – he just had the misfortune to be in charge when the Second World War broke out. In his two full seasons in charge, he led United to 12th in the Second Division in 1931–32 and to 14th in Division One in 1938–39, with an overall win ratio of 39.5 per cent. In fact, his real role at United was club secretary, where he had been involved since the early 1930s, helping new chairman James Gibson get United back on its feet after the latter had saved it from possible bankruptcy. On the playing side, his other most notable achievement was to help found MUJAC (Manchester United Junior Athletic Club) in 1938; this body provided the basis of United's scouting set-up that Matt Busby used so effectively after the war. Crickmer remained as club secretary up until his death in the Munich Air Disaster on 6 February 1958.

★Two spells: October 1945 to May 1969, and December 1970 to June 1971.
†Two spells: April 1931 to August 1932, and October 1937 to October 1945.

UNITED PLAYERS WITH MOST LEAGUE
TITLE MEDALS

	Player	Seasons	Total
1	Ryan Giggs	1992–93 to 2010–11	12
2	Paul Scholes	1995–96 to 2010–11	10
3	Gary Neville	1995–96 to 2008–09	8
4	Denis Irwin	1992–93 to 2000–01	7
4	Roy Keane	1993–94 to 2002–03	7
6	David Beckham	1995–96 to 2002–03	6
6	**Nicky Butt**	**1995–96 to 2002–03**	**6**
6	Phil Neville	1995–96 to 2002–03	6
6	Ole Gunnar Solskjaer	1996–97 to 2006–07	6

Rio Ferdinand is the only current player, with five titles, closest to joining this list. But what is often forgotten when looking back over the great players who emerged from the famous Class of 92 is that, Ryan Giggs apart, the first one really to establish himself in the side was Nicky Butt. Along with David Beckham and Gary Neville, he made his debut in the team in 1992–93, but in 1994–95 he appeared in 35 of 59 games, while Gary Neville managed 27, Scholes 25, Beckham ten and Phil Neville just three. A local lad, he fulfilled the quiet but essential midfielder's role of breaking up opposition moves and then passing the ball to a team-mate to go on and create something. It doesn't earn you too many headlines, but you can understand why early in 1995–96 Alex Ferguson stated he had the best midfield pairing in the league in Butt and Roy Keane. He played 387 games for United before leaving his boyhood club for Newcastle United in the summer of 2004, signing off with an FA Cup victory over Millwall to add to his medal collection.

UNITED PLAYERS BORN IN AFRICA, ASIA AND AUSTRALIA

	Player	Country	Debut	Apps (Goals)
1	Charlie Mitten	Burma	31 August 1946	162 (61)
2	Mark Bosnich	Australia	30 April 1990	38
3	Quinton Fortune	South Africa	30 August 1999	126 (11)
4	Eric Djemba-Djemba	Cameroon	10 August 2003	39 (2)
5	Ji-Sung Park	South Korea	9 August 2005	177 (24)
6	Dong Fangzhuo	China	9 May 2007	3
7	Manucho	Angola	23 September 2008	3
8	Mame Biram Diouf	Senegal	9 January 2010	6 (1)

Having been born in Rangoon, Charlie Mitten joined United before the war but did not make his debut until August 1946. From February 1948 to the end of the 1949–50 season, he played in 114 consecutive games at outside-left. A pacy winger, he was unerring in his delivery of the ball and had plenty of tricks up his sleeve, too. He was a prolific goalscorer in an era when many wingers were there mainly to supply chances. Mitten was also one of the most reliable penalty-takers in the business. His secret: 'Aim always for the corners of the goal.' In March 1950, he scored three penalties against Aston Villa – all of them went in at the same corner, even after the keeper asked where the final one was going. Part of the FA Cup-winning side of 1948, he was lured to play for Santa Fé in Colombia while United were touring in the USA during the summer of 1950. Their offer of £50 per week was far more than it was possible to earn in England at the time, because of the maximum wage. But that was how 'Cheeky Charlie' became the 'Bogotà Bandit', and so ended the United career of one of the club's best-ever wingers.

MOST RECENT PLAYERS TO APPEAR IN
EVERY LEAGUE MATCH

	Player	Appearances (Sub)	Season
1	Patrice Evra	37 (1)	2009–10
2	Edwin van der Sar	38	2005–06
3	Gary Pallister	42	1994–95
4	Denis Irwin	42	1993–94
5	Steve Bruce	42	1992–93
5	Brian McClair	41 (1)	1992–93
5	Gary Pallister	42	1992–93
5	Peter Schmeichel	42	1992–93
9	Brian McClair	41 (1)	1991–92
10	Mike Phelan	38	1989–90

French left-back Patrice Evra became the first United outfield
player in 15 years to play in every Premier League match during the
2009–10 campaign. Signed from Monaco early in 2006, he made
his debut on 14 January away to City in the local derby. After a difficult first half, he was substituted at the break as United went on
to lose. Since then, however, he has rarely put a foot wrong,
coming on as a late substitute in the 2006 Carling Cup final to pick
up the first of eight honours for the Reds by the end of the
2010–11 season, including the Champions League title in 2008.
During United's injury-hit campaign in 2009–10, he was the one
defender who remained fit throughout and so ensured he kept control of the dressing-room music system. Now widely regarded as
one of the best left-backs in the world, as good going forward as he
is in defence, he has endeared himself to Reds everywhere by the
way he has immersed himself in the history of the club.

BIGGEST DEFEATS IN THE PREMIER LEAGUE

	Opposition	Venue	Date	Score
1	Newcastle United	St James' Park	20 October 1996	5–0
1	Chelsea	Stamford Bridge	3 October 1999	5–0
3	**Southampton**	**The Dell**	**26 October 1996**	**6–3**
4	Tottenham Hotspur	White Hart Lane	1 January 1996	4–1
4	Manchester City	Eastlands	13 March 2004	4–1
4	Middlesbrough	Riverside Stadium	29 October 2005	4–1
4	Liverpool	Old Trafford	14 March 2009	4–1

This list of big defeats is a satisfyingly short one. It wasn't until 3 April 2010 that United lost their 100th game in the history of the Premier League. Their nearest rivals, Arsenal, reached the same landmark as early as 10 September 2005. Only once in Premier League history have United ever conceded six goals – and it came just six days after they had lost 5–0 to Newcastle at St James' Park. At The Dell, United fell behind early on to an Eyal Berkovic goal, but the sending off of Roy Keane for two bookable offences completely changed the dynamics of the game. In his memoirs, he said that he put in 'a rash challenge or a crunching tackle' to get his team-mates fired up, feeling that everyone was 'going through the motions'. Matt Le Tissier doubled the Saints' lead with a superb chip over Peter Schmeichel from the edge of the box before David Beckham pulled back a goal for the team in blue and white (no grey shirts this time). With less than ten minutes to go, it was still 3–2 to Southampton, but as United tired, suddenly the floodgates opened and the final scoreline ended up a very flattering one to the South Coast team. Fortunately, United bounced back after their blip and won the title by seven points from Newcastle.

MOST CAPS BEFORE THE FIRST WORLD WAR

	Player	Country	Teams	Caps
1	Billy Meredith	Wales	Manchester C, Manchester U	45
2	Bob Crompton	England	Blackburn Rovers	41
3	Olphert Stanfield	Ireland	Distillery	30
4	Bobby Walker	Scotland	Hearts	29
5	Charlie Morris	Wales	Chirk, Derby Co, Huddersfield T	27
5	Billy Lewis	Wales	Bangor, Crewe A, Chester, Mcr C	27
5	Robert Milne	Ireland	Linfield	27
8	Billy Wedlock	England	Bristol City	26
8	Sam Torrans	Ireland	Linfield	26
10	Billy Scott	Ireland	Linfield, Everton, Leeds City	25

Nowadays, it is possible for a player to win at least ten caps in a year, but before the First World War almost all internationals in Britain were played between England, Scotland, Wales and Ireland (in those days, the island had not split into two countries), meaning it was almost impossible to win more than three in a year. So for someone to win even 25 caps was very rare. All of which makes the feat of star United winger Billy Meredith even more impressive. Without a doubt, he was the George Best, the Ryan Giggs, the Cristiano Ronaldo of his era. He made his debut for United on 1 January 1907, having been signed from neighbours City. He had an instant impact, setting up the only goal in a 1–0 win over Aston Villa. The charismatic winger helped inspire United in their first great era, winning three trophies by 1911. He was instrumental in early work to set up a players' union, and would continue playing for United until 1921, when he returned to City to finish his career.

CHAMPIONS LEAGUE FINAL GOALSCORERS

	Player	Opposition	Date	Time
1	Bobby Charlton	Benfica	29 May 1968	53
2	George Best	Benfica	29 May 1968	93
3	Brian Kidd	Benfica	29 May 1968	94
4	Bobby Charlton	Benfica	29 May 1968	99
5	Teddy Sheringham	Bayern Munich	26 May 1999	90+1
6	Ole Gunnar Solskjaer	Bayern Munich	26 May 1999	90+3
7	Cristiano Ronaldo	Chelsea	21 May 2008	26
8	Wayne Rooney	Barcelona	28 May 2011	34

In 1968, Bobby Charlton became the first player to score a goal for United in the final of the European Cup, and by the end of the game he had become the first – and remains the only – man ever to score twice for the Reds in the biggest match in European football. It was entirely appropriate that he should have this honour, as he had made his European debut 11 years previously, in April 1957, at the end of United's first campaign in Europe, scoring against the masters of the tournament, Real Madrid. The following season, he had been part of the side that suffered in the Munich Air Disaster. Just as it was for Matt Busby, the quest for the European Cup was motivated in part by the desire to do right by those who had lost their lives. Captain on the night, Charlton gave United the lead when he headed precisely home from a David Sadler left-wing cross eight minutes into the second half. Then, in extra time, he made things safe at 4–1 when Brian Kidd found him on the corner of the six-yard box. Ten years on from Munich, Charlton felt, 'It was triumph and deliverance all wrapped into one.'

MOST RECENT SIR MATT BUSBY
PLAYERS OF THE YEAR

	Player	Season
1	Javier Hernandez	2010–11
2	Wayne Rooney	2009–10
3	Nemanja Vidic	2008–09
4	Cristiano Ronaldo	2007–08
5	Cristiano Ronaldo	2006–07
6	Wayne Rooney	2005–06
7	**Gabriel Heinze**	**2004–05**
8	Cristiano Ronaldo	2003–04
9	Ruud van Nistelrooy	2002–03
10	Ruud van Nistelrooy	2001–02

In recent years the Sir Matt Busby Player of the Year award, voted for by United fans, has tended to go to forwards. Cristiano Ronaldo is the only player ever to have won it three times since Brian McClair was the first recipient back in 1988. Argentinian international full-back Gabriel Heinze became only the second defender to pick up the award (Gary Pallister was the first, in 1990) after his whole-hearted and committed displays in what was, in truth, a disappointing campaign for the Reds. He was 26 when he joined United in the summer of 2004 for a fee of about £7 million, having proved a great success at Paris St Germain. Despite his efforts that season, the Reds ended up 18 points behind champions Chelsea (the biggest gap since 1991) and he missed out on playing in the FA Cup final against Arsenal, which United lost on penalties. The following season, he sustained a serious injury against Villarreal, which prompted Sir Alex Ferguson to sign Patrice Evra. He was eventually sold to Real Madrid in 2007.

MOST GOALS IN THE FA CUP

	Player	Career	Appearances	Goals
1	Denis Law	1962–73	46	34
2	Jack Rowley	1937–55	42	26
3	George Best	1963–74	46	21
3	Stan Pearson	1937–53	30	21
5	Bobby Charlton	1956–73	78	19
6	Mark Hughes	1983–95	46	17
7	David Herd	1961–68	35	15
8	Brian McClair	1987–98	45	14
8	Ruud van Nistelrooy	2001–06	14	14
10	Cristiano Ronaldo	2003–09	26	13
10	Paul Scholes	1994–2011	41	13

Jack Rowley was United's great post-war centre-forward, but had actually joined the club for a fee of £3,000 in October 1937 from Bournemouth. A combative and abrasive character, on and off the pitch, he had to wait until the 1945–46 season to score his first FA Cup goals for United, against Accrington Stanley. But it was in the 1948 and 1949 FA Cup runs that he had his greatest days. Having scored goals in the third, fourth and sixth rounds, Rowley was United's key threat in the 1948 Cup final against Blackpool. After the Reds went a goal down, he nipped in between the hesitating Tangerines defence to score the equaliser. When United fell behind again, it was Rowley who came to the rescue once more, and set them on their way to a famous 4–2 victory. On 12 February 1949, Yeovil Town felt the full force of 'Gunner' Rowley, who hit five goals as United won 8–0 in front of a crowd of 81,565.

THE TEAMS UNITED HAVE FACED
ONLY ONCE★

	Opposition	Date	Tournament	Result
1	Hartlepool United	5 January 1957	FA Cup 3rd	4–3
2	Aldershot	9 September 1970	League Cup 2nd	3–1
3	Peterborough United	24 January 1976	FA Cup 4th	3–1
4	Tranmere Rovers	1 September 1976	League Cup 2nd	5–0
5	Rochdale	9 January 1986	FA Cup 3rd	2–0
6	Hereford United	28 January 1990	FA Cup 4th	1–0
7	Barnet	26 October 2005	League Cup 3rd	4–1
8	**Southend United**	**7 November 2006**	**League Cup 4th**	**0–1**
9	Scunthorpe United	22 September 2010	League Cup 3rd	5–2
10	Crawley Town	19 February 2011	FA Cup 5th	1–0

While Hartlepool have waited the longest for a re-match, and have boasted three former Reds as their manager in the interim (Allenby Chilton in 1962–63, David McCreery in 1994–95 and Chris Turner, 1999–2002 and 2008–10), only Southend can boast a 100 per cent record against United. It was an embarrassing night for the Carling Cup holders United at Roots Hall. Freddy Eastwood put the Essex side in the lead after 27 minutes with a fantastic 30-yard free kick, curled round the wall into the top corner. As usual in the early rounds, Sir Alex had given opportunities to some fringe players in his squad, but United still fielded a starting line-up that included ten internationals, among them Cristiano Ronaldo and Wayne Rooney. Numerous chances fell United's way to get back into the game, but keeper Darryl Flahavan was in fine form to deny them every time. It was not the way Sir Alex wanted to mark 20 years in charge at Old Trafford.

★Includes all teams in the Football League during 2011–12.

CHAMPIONS LEAGUE VICTORIES IN GERMANY, ITALY AND SPAIN

	Opponents	Date	Round	Score
1	ASK Vorwaerts	17 November 1965	1st Round	2–0
2	Juventus	21 April 1999	Semi-final	3–2
3	Deportivo La Coruna	2 April 2002	Quarter-final	2–0
4	Bayer Leverkusen	24 September 2002	Group Stage	2–1
5	Juventus	25 February 2003	Group Stage	3–0
6	Roma	1 April 2008	Quarter-final	2–0
7	Wolfsburg	8 December 2009	Group Stage	3–1
8	AC Milan	16 February 2010	2nd Round	3–2
9	Valencia	29 September 2010	Group Stage	1–0
10	Schalke 04	26 April 2011	Semi-final	2–0

In all of United's Champions League history, they have won away only ten times in the tournament's three most successful countries: four times in Italy (out of 15), four times in Germany (out of 12) and twice in Spain (out of 15). The most crucial victory came against Juventus in 1999 to secure a place in the final. Having drawn 1–1 at Old Trafford, United knew they needed a high-scoring draw or a win in Turin. Filippo Inzaghi scored twice in the first ten minutes to leave United all but out of the tournament, against a side also featuring Didier Deschamps, Edgar Davids and Zinedine Zidane. Midway through the first half, Roy Keane pulled back a goal and drove on his team in the most inspirational act of leadership seen since Bryan Robson's against Barcelona in 1984. What made his efforts all the more remarkable was that he was booked and knew he would miss the final. One goal wasn't enough, but Dwight Yorke scored the equaliser before half-time, before Andrew Cole wrapped things up on 84 minutes.

BIGGEST DEFEATS

	Opposition	Venue	Date	Comp	Score
1	Blackburn Rovers	Ewood Park	10 April 1926	Div 1	7–0
1	Aston Villa	Villa Park	27 December 1930	Div 1	7–0
1	Wolverhampton W	Molineux	26 December 1931	Div 2	7–0
4	Stoke City	Victoria Ground	7 January 1893	Div 1	7–1
4	Liverpool	Anfield	12 October 1895	Div 2	7–1
4	Burnley	Turf Moor	13 February 1901	FAC 1	7–1
4	Aston Villa	Villa Park	26 February 1910	Div 1	7–1
4	**Newcastle United**	**Old Trafford**	**10 September 1927**	**Div 1**	**7–1**
4	Charlton Athletic	The Valley	11 February 1939	Div 1	7–1

The good news from this list is that not one of United's biggest defeats has taken place since the Second World War. Since 1945 their worst results have been two 6–0 reverses (at Leicester City in Division One on 21 January 1961 and at Ipswich Town in Division One on 1 March 1980). Only one of the Reds' worst performances came at Old Trafford, back in 1927–28. That campaign was an extraordinary one, as just seven points separated Derby County, who finished fourth with 44 points, from Middlesbrough, who were 22nd and bottom with 37. United ended up with 39 points, and were saved from relegation only by winning their last three games of the season, including a 6–1 defeat of Liverpool on the final day. On that September day, United went into the fifth game of the season unbeaten under new manager Herbert Bamlett, but it all went horribly wrong for them against the Magpies. Joe Spence scored United's only goal, but it was little consolation to the 50,217 fans in Old Trafford – the biggest league crowd of the season, many of whom clearly decided not to return.

BIGGEST WINS

	Opposition	Venue	Date	Comp	Score
1	Anderlecht	Maine Road	26 September 1956	EC Pr	10–0
2	Wolverhampton W	North Road	15 October 1892	Div 1	10–1
3	Walsall	Bank Street	3 April 1895	Div 2	9–0
3	Darwen	Bank Street	24 December 1898	Div 2	9–0
3	Ipswich Town	Old Trafford	4 March 1995	PL	9–0
6	Yeovil Town	Maine Road	12 February 1949	FAC 5	8–0
7	Queens Park Rangers	Old Trafford	19 March 1969	Div 1	8–1
7	Nottingham Forest	City Ground	6 February 1999	PL	8–1

United have also had eight 7–0 victories in their history. However, the club's biggest win came in its first-ever 'home' European game, which had to be played at Maine Road as floodlights had not yet been installed at Old Trafford. Manager Matt Busby had had to battle to persuade the Football League to allow United to compete in the tournament at all, but he wanted to test out his young stars against the best Europe had to offer. The Belgian champions had been beaten 2–0 in Anderlecht, but there were still some nerves ahead of the return leg. After some heavy rain, the pitch was muddy, but United put in what Busby called 'the finest exhibition of teamwork I had ever seen'. In some ways, the star of the occasion was David Pegg – even though he did not score, he was involved in setting up most of the goals. Tommy Taylor scored the first inside ten minutes, then added a second before Dennis Viollet hit a hat-trick to give United a 5–0 half-time lead. In the second half, Taylor completed his hat-trick, Viollet added a fourth, while Eddie Colman scored two and Johnny Berry one. United had announced that they meant business in Europe.

ALL-TIME PREMIER LEAGUE TABLE

	Team	P	W	D	L	Pts	Ave Pts
1	Manchester United	734	472	158	104	1574	2.14
2	Arsenal	734	394	197	143	1379	1.88
3	Chelsea	734	383	189	162	1338	1.82
4	Liverpool	734	366	184	184	1282	1.75
5	Aston Villa	734	276	223	235	1051	1.43
6	Tottenham Hotspur	734	274	195	265	1017	1.39
7	Everton	734	257	207	270	978	1.33
8	Newcastle United	654	258	178	218	952	1.46
9	Blackburn Rovers	658	254	177	227	939	1.43
10	West Ham United	616	202	158	256	764	1.24

Manchester City sit 11th in this list, with 695 points, while Leeds United (with 1.48) have the highest points average of any side outside the Top 10. What these figures mean is that in an average 38-game season, United achieved just over 81 points, while their nearest challengers Arsenal achieved just over 71 points. In that sense, the most 'typical' season for the two clubs came in 2000–01, when United finished top of the table (for the third consecutive year) with 80 points, and Arsenal were runners-up with 70. This was the last season when the core of the Treble-winning side still played together. Goalkeeper Fabien Barthez was the only major new recruit that year, while Teddy Sheringham had his most prolific season for United, scoring 15 goals in the Premier League, and became the FWA Footballer of the Year. The title was secured as early as 14 April, with a 4–2 home win over Coventry City, with five games to spare. But the true scale of United's dominance was shown by their 6–1 hammering of Arsenal in February.

60 APPEARANCES IN A SEASON

	Player	Season	Total Poss	Total Played (plus sub)
1	Steve Bruce	1993–94	63	61 (1)
1	Denis Irwin	1993–94	63	61 (1)
3	Gary Pallister	1993–94	63	61
4	Shay Brennan	1964–65	60	60
4	John Connelly	1964–65	60	60
4	Tony Dunne	1964–65	60	60
4	Bill Foulkes	1964–65	60	60
4	Mike Duxbury	1982–83	60	60
4	Peter Schmeichel	1993–94	63	60

Just nine men have played 60 or more games in a season for United, a list that seems unlikely to increase in today's era of squad rotation. Four of them played in the 1964–65 season and another four in the 1993–94 campaign. However, Mike Duxbury was the only man to be ever-present in 1982–83. The Accrington-born defender and midfielder was a very adaptable player, capable of lining up in most positions, like John O'Shea recently, but was probably most effective at right-back. Having come through the youth ranks, he made his debut for United in August 1980, but it was only in 1982–83 that he became an automatic pick. He featured in all 42 league matches, seven FA Cup ties (helping United win that trophy in a replay against Brighton), nine League Cup fixtures (where United also reached the final) and two UEFA Cup matches. He managed just one goal, in a 4–0 win against Notts County, and his form earned him an England call-up the following season. After a decade of service, he left for Blackburn Rovers on a free transfer in the summer of 1990.

MOST SUCCESSFUL UNITED MANAGERS*

		Career	Matches Played	Win Ratio
1	Sir Alex Ferguson	1986–	1392	59.20%
2	**Ernest Mangnall**	**1903–12**	**373**	**54.16%**
3	Sir Matt Busby†	1945–71	1141	50.48%
4	Ron Atkinson	1981–86	292	50.00%
5	Tommy Docherty	1972–77	228	46.93%
6	John Bentley	1912–14	82	43.90%
7	James West	1900–03	113	40.71%
8	Dave Sexton	1977–81	201	40.30%
9	Walter Crickmer†	1931–45	119	39.50%
10	Scott Duncan	1932–37	235	39.15%

The three men who top this list are the only ones ever to have managed United to league title success. Ernest Mangnall deserves his place, as he was undoubtedly one of the greatest managers United ever had. Educated at Bolton Grammar School, he joined the club from Burnley in the autumn of 1903. When Mangnall took charge, United were in Division Two, their usual home at that stage. But he soon changed all that. A strict disciplinarian, he knew how to motivate a side and had a great eye for a player. It was not until 1906 that he finally won promotion. By 1908 United were champions of England, in 1909 they won the FA Cup for the first time, and in 1911, a year after moving to their smart new stadium at Old Trafford, they were champions again. If he had not done so well, it is doubtful the stadium would ever have been built. Sadly, in 1912, he moved across to Manchester City, but he had created a legacy at United that lasts to this day.

*In terms of the highest percentage of wins; †Both these men were in charge for two spells (see page 135 for details).

TEAMS WITH THE WORST DEFENCE AGAINST UNITED

	Opponent	Goals Conceded	Games	Average
1	Wigan Athletic	41	13	3.15
2	Loughborough Town	29	10	2.90
3	Burton Swifts	36	14	2.57
4	Glossop	34	14	2.43
5	Burton United	29	12	2.42
6	Walsall	40	17	2.35
7	Luton Town	90	39	2.31
8	Millwall	34	14	2.29
9	Darwen	27	12	2.25
10	Port Vale	97	45	2.16

Most of the teams in the list above were more familiar foes in United's early days, but that is not true of Wigan Athletic. In fact, the Reds had never faced them until December 2005, after the Latics had finally made their way to the top of the football pyramid to join the Premier League in 2005–06. In that first game, Wigan were brushed aside 4–0, with Rio Ferdinand starting the onslaught as he headed home a Ryan Giggs corner after 30 minutes. Amazingly, in 140 appearances for the Reds since his record-breaking transfer from Leeds United in the summer of 2002, it was his first goal for the club. Wayne Rooney hit two more either side of half-time, before Ruud van Nistelrooy rounded off the scoring with a penalty. To date, United have a 100 per cent record against Wigan, with Rooney in particular enjoying his games against them – he has scored ten goals past various Wigan keepers. United's biggest wins against Wigan, 5–0, came home and away in the 2009–10 season.

MOST APPEARANCES FOR UNITED
BY ENGLISH PLAYERS

	Player	Career	Appearances
1	Bobby Charlton	1956–73	758
2	Bill Foulkes	1952–69	688
3	Paul Scholes	1994–2011	676
4	Gary Neville	1992–2011	602
5	Alex Stepney	1966–78	539
6	Joe Spence	1919–33	510
7	Bryan Robson	1981–94	461
8	**Jack Silcock**	**1919–34**	**449**
9	Gary Pallister	1989–98	437
10	Jack Rowley	1937–55	424

Steve Bruce (414) is the only other Englishman to have made 400–plus appearances for United and, unlike all of the above, was never capped by his country. Fellow defender Jack Silcock did not have much more luck with the England selectors, appearing just three times between 1921 and 1923. Born in Wigan on 15 January 1898, he was destined for a career in the mines until manager John Robson spotted him playing for Atherton during the First World War and snapped up the teenager. He made his official debut for United in the first game after the war, and was a regular in the side for 15 years. The full-back had good distribution skills, but he played in what were generally poor sides as United struggled to find any consistency at this time. At the end of the 1933–34 season, at the age of 36 and struggling to get into the team, he left the club for Oldham. It gives some idea of the state United were in at the time that this was seen as a step up.

MOST GOALS FOR UNITED BY
ENGLISH PLAYERS

	Player	Career	Goals
1	Bobby Charlton	1956–73	249
2	Jack Rowley	1937–55	211
3	Dennis Viollet	1953–61	179
4	Joe Spence	1919–33	168
5	Paul Scholes	1994–2011	150
6	**Stan Pearson**	**1937–53**	**148**
7	Wayne Rooney	2004–	147
8	Tommy Taylor	1953–58	131
9	Andrew Cole	1995–2001	121
10	George Wall	1906–15	100

Salford lad Stan Pearson made his United debut as an 18-year-old in November 1937, but within two years his career was interrupted by the war, where he saw service in India. Along with Johnny Carey and Jack Rowley, he became a central part of Matt Busby's plans for the club when he joined in 1945. A skilful and creative inside-forward, Pearson was a gentleman on and off the pitch, his style complementing the more robust Rowley. However, that did not hold him back from scoring goals. In each of the seven post-war seasons in which he featured for the Reds, he never scored fewer than 17 goals in a campaign, with his best season coming in 1947–48. Then, he was on particularly fine form in the FA Cup. Having scored a hat-trick in the 3–1 semi-final victory over Derby County, his goal ten minutes from time in the final gave United a lead against Blackpool for the first time. After leaving the club, he played on at Bury and then Chester, continuing at the latter past his 40th birthday.

UNITED'S FIRST TEN HAT-TRICKS IN THE PREMIER LEAGUE

	Player	Opponents	Date	Score
1	Andrei Kanchelskis	Manchester City	10 November 1994	5–0
2	Andrew Cole (5)	Ipswich Town	4 March 1995	9–0
3	Andrew Cole	Barnsley	25 October 1997	7–0
4	Dwight Yorke	Leicester City	16 January 1999	6–2
5	**Ole Gunnar Solskjaer (4)**	**Nottingham Forest**	**6 February 1999**	**8–1**
6	Andrew Cole (4)	Newcastle United	30 August 1999	5–1
7	Ole Gunnar Solskjaer (4)	Everton	4 December 1999	5–1
8	Dwight Yorke	Derby County	11 March 2000	3–1
9	Paul Scholes	West Ham United	1 April 2000	7–1
10	Teddy Sheringham	Southampton	28 October 2000	5–0

All hat-tricks for Manchester United are special, but the one scored by Ole Gunnar Solskjaer in February 1999 takes some beating. That season the Norwegian often found himself coming off the bench, rather than starting. With Andrew Cole, Teddy Sheringham and Dwight Yorke all competing up front, the club had formidable options. Between them, they scored 76 goals in 1998–99. On this occasion, Solskjaer came on late in the second half for Yorke with the game safely won at 4–1. Before going on, Jim Ryan said to him: 'We don't need any more goals – just keep the ball. Play nice and simple.' Ole clearly wasn't listening, as he added a fifth on 80 minutes, tapping in a Gary Neville cross. He followed it up by beating Dave Beasant one-on-one after 87 minutes and hammered home his hat-trick after 89, before rounding it off on 90 minutes from Paul Scholes' horrendous miscue. The final score of 8–1 remains a record away victory in the Premier League and completed a miserable day for former Reds boss Ron Atkinson, the Forest manager.

ENGLAND GAMES AT OLD TRAFFORD

	Opposition	Date	Score	United Players
1	Scotland	17 April 1926	0–1	–
2	Ireland	16 November 1938	7–0	–
3	South Africa	24 May 1997	2–1	Beckham, Butt, P. Neville, Scholes
4	Greece	6 October 2001	2–2	Beckham (1), Cole, G. Neville, Scholes
5	Sweden	10 November 2001	1–1	Beckham (1), Butt, G. Neville, P. Neville, Scholes
6	Liechtenstein	10 September 2003	2–0	G. Neville, P. Neville
7	Denmark	16 November 2003	2–3	Butt, G. Neville, P. Neville
8	Wales	9 October 2004	2–0	Ferdinand, G. Neville, Rooney, Smith
9	Northern Ireland	26 March 2005	4–0	Ferdinand, G. Neville, Rooney
10	Austria	8 October 2005	1–0	Ferdinand, Richardson
11	Poland	12 October 2005	2–1	Ferdinand, Rooney, Smith
12	Hungary	30 May 2006	3–1	Ferdinand, G. Neville
13	Jamaica	3 June 2006	6–0	Ferdinand
14	Greece	16 August 2006	4–0	Ferdinand, G. Neville, Richardson
15	Andorra	2 September 2006	5–0	Brown, Richardson
16	Macedonia	7 October 2006	0–0	Carrick, G. Neville, Rooney
17	Spain	7 February 2007	0–1	Carrick, Ferdinand, Foster, G. Neville

England have a good record at Old Trafford, but without doubt the most dramatic game was the final World Cup qualifier in October 2001, when England needed at least a draw against Greece to guarantee qualification. David Beckham's last-minute 30-yard free kick secured the vital point. He remains the only United player ever to have scored for England at the ground, both his goals coming in successive games.

MOST COMMON EUROPEAN OPPONENTS

	Opponent	Period	Times Met
1	Juventus	1976–2003	12
2	Barcelona	1984–2011	11
3	AC Milan	1958–2010	10
4	Bayern Munich	1998–2010	9
5	Porto	1977–2009	8
5	Real Madrid	1957–2003	8
5	Valencia	1982–2010	8
8	Benfica	1966–2006	7

Although United have met Juventus more often, there is no doubt that it is Barcelona who have been the Reds' most significant opponents in Europe, the two sides having met in the semi-finals of the 2008 Champions League and also in three European finals: the 1991 European Cup-Winners' Cup final, and the 2009 and 2011 Champions League finals. While the latter two games ended in defeat, the first final was a brilliant success, as United took on a Barca side that would go on to win the European Cup the following season. United were well on top in Rotterdam but couldn't score until the 67th minute. A Bryan Robson free kick was headed towards goal by Steve Bruce, only for ex-Barca player Mark Hughes to bundle it over the line. A few minutes later, Hughes was put through one-on-one with the keeper Carlos Busquets (father of Sergio). He skipped round the challenge but took the ball out wide to the edge of the area, level with the six-yard box. However, from that tight angle he slammed home a brilliant goal, past two defenders tracking back. There was still time for a late fightback by Barca, but United won through 2–1.

BIGGEST WINS IN THE CHAMPIONS LEAGUE*

	Opposition	Venue	Date	Round	Score
1	Anderlecht	Maine Road	26 September 1956	Prel	10–0
2	Waterford	Old Trafford	2 October 1968	1st	7–1
2	**Roma**	**Old Trafford**	**10 April 2007**	**QF**	**7–1**
4	Shamrock Rovers	Dalymount Park	25 September 1957	Prel	6–0
4	HJK Helsinki	Old Trafford	6 October 1965	Prel	6–0
6	Brondby	Old Trafford	4 November 1998	Gp	5–0
6	Zalaegerszeg	Old Trafford	27 August 2002	Qual	5–0
6	Panathinaikos	Old Trafford	16 September 2003	Gp	5–0
9	Brondby	Parken	21 October 1998	Gp	6–2
9	Fenerbahce	Old Trafford	28 September 2004	Gp	6–2

United's crushing victory over Roma stands out in this list. The other wins were all in the early stages of the tournament, but this one took place six days after United had lost 2–1 in the Olympic Stadium when there was a place in the semi-finals at stake. Roma had conceded just five goals in their nine Champions League fixtures to that point and would finish runners-up in Serie A. The 74,476 fans packed into Old Trafford, and millions watching on TV, were expecting a tense evening. Inside 11 minutes Michael Carrick had run on to a ball laid into his path by Cristiano Ronaldo and lashed it home from 25 yards. Seven minutes later it was three, as Alan Smith and Wayne Rooney got in on the act. Ronaldo added two more either side of half-time, before Carrick hit another stunner into the top corner from outside the box. Even Patrice Evra, popping up in the inside-right position, scored. Watching on, an impressed Edwin van der Sar commented: 'I have never seen a performance like this in my life.'

*Including European Cup and Champions League qualifiers.

MOST LEAGUE GAMES UNDEFEATED
FROM THE START OF A SEASON

	Season	Games Played	Division	Final Position
1	2010–11	24	Prem Lg	1st
2	1985–86	15	First	4th
3	1991–92	12	First	2nd
3	1956–57	12	First	1st
5	1974–75	9	Second	1st
5	1996–97	9	Prem Lg	1st
5	1999–2000	9	Prem Lg	1st
8	1984–85	8	First	4th
8	1949–50	8	First	4th
8	1997–98	8	Prem Lg	2nd

In 1985–86, United had a stunning start to their season, winning the first ten games of the campaign. In that time, only three sides had managed even to score against the Reds, while United banged in 27 goals. A couple of draws in the next five games, including one against title rivals Liverpool, still left the club with 41 points out of 45, and ten clear of the men from Anfield. Mark Hughes was in devastating form up front, scoring ten goals in this period, and all around him was a very settled side. Captain Bryan Robson was at his peak, and manager Ron Atkinson seemed to have found the key to deliver the title back to United. The first defeat came at Hillsborough against Sheffield Wednesday on 9 November by 1–0. Significantly, Robson's hamstring problem prevented him from completing the game, and he missed most of the next four months through injury. Others also picked up injuries, so that only five of the squad played 30 or more league games that season and United's title challenge fizzled out.

MOST APPEARANCES BY SIR ALEX
FERGUSON'S SIGNINGS

	Player	Career	Appearances	Goals
1	Denis Irwin	1990–2002	529	33
2	Roy Keane	1993–2005	480	51
3	Brian McClair	1987–98	471	127
4	Gary Pallister	1989–98	437	15
5	Steve Bruce	1987–96	414	51
6	Peter Schmeichel	1991–99	398	1
7	Ole Gunnar Solskjaer	1996–2007	366	126
8	Mikael Silvestre	1999–2007	361	10
9	Rio Ferdinand	2002–	360	7
10	Wayne Rooney	2004–	322	147

The question of who has been the best signing made by Sir Alex in his time at United will always be a hot topic of debate, and most of those in this list would have to be candidates for that award. Full-back Denis Irwin certainly provided value for money in anyone's book, each of his appearances costing the equivalent of just £1,181. He was signed by United in the summer of 1990 for a fee of £625,000, after impressing for Oldham Athletic, who met the Reds in two FA Cup semi-finals the previous April. The Irish international made his debut in the Charity Shield in August 1990, and was a model of consistency throughout the 1990s, making his final appearance for the Reds in the last game of the 2001–02 season. He won seven Premier League titles in his time at United. A brilliant professional, equally at home on either flank, he played for 21 seasons in all: starting with three years at Leeds, four at Oldham and finishing with two at Wolves.

THE TEAM FOR THE RETURN TO OLD TRAFFORD

	Player	Career	Appearances	Goals
1	Jack Crompton	1946–55	212	0
2	Johnny Carey	1937–53	344	17
3	John Aston Sr	1946–54	284	30
4	**Jack Warner**	**1938–50**	**116**	**2**
5	Sammy Lynn	1948–49	13	0
6	Henry Cockburn	1946–54	275	4
7	Jimmy Delaney	1946–50	184	28
8	John Downie	1949–53	116	37
9	Jack Rowley	1937–55	424	211
10	Stan Pearson	1937–53	343	148
11	Charlie Mitten	1946–50	162	61

When United were finally able to return to action at Old Trafford on 24 August 1949 to take on Bolton Wanderers, a crowd of 41,748 came to see the Reds record a 3–0 win, with goals from Charlie Mitten, Jack Rowley and an own goal. It was just two days short of ten years since the previous first-team game at the famous stadium, as the ground had suffered serious bomb damage in March 1941 during the Second World War. Just four of the team that lined up that day had played there in its pre-war guise: Carey, Pearson, Rowley and Warner. Of that quartet, it is Jack Warner who is probably the least familiar name. The Welsh international had been signed from Swansea before the war and was nearing his 38th birthday at the time. The right-half had an aggressive temperament, rarely ducking a challenge on or off the pitch. He soon moved on to Oldham before ending his career as player-manager at Rochdale.

BIGGEST WINS IN THE FIRST DIVISION

	Opposition	Venue	Date	Score
1	Wolverhampton W	North Road	15 October 1892	10–1
2	Queens Park Rangers	Old Trafford	19 March 1969	8–1
3	Aston Villa	Old Trafford	8 March 1950	7–0
3	**Aston Villa**	**Old Trafford**	**24 October 1964**	**7–0**
3	West Bromwich Albion	Old Trafford	8 April 1970	7–0
6	Derby County	North Road	31 December 1892	7–1
7	Huddersfield Town	Old Trafford	5 November 1949	6–0
7	Huddersfield Town	Old Trafford	28 April 1951	6–0
7	Leeds United	Old Trafford	9 September 1959	6–0
7	Blackpool	Bloomfield Road	27 February 1960	6–0
7	Chelsea	Old Trafford	26 December 1960	6–0
7	Burnley	Old Trafford	12 April 1961	6–0
7	Newcastle United	Old Trafford	4 May 1968	6–0

Of all United's wins by a six-goal margin or more in the First Division, only one came in a title-winning season – against Aston Villa in the autumn of 1964. It came in the middle of a run of 11 successive victories when United scored an astonishing 39 goals, and Denis Law was responsible for a third of that total. On the day, Law scored four goals, David Herd two and new signing John Connelly got the other one. For many older fans, that season still resonates as one when the Reds played their most free-flowing football, with an incredibly settled line-up that almost invariably read: Pat Dunne, Brennan, Tony Dunne, Crerand, Foulkes, Stiles, Connelly, Charlton, Herd, Law, Best. Despite all that, it was a very close-fought race with Leeds, but United just won through.

MOST LEAGUE TITLES

	Team	Period	Wins
1	Manchester United	1908–2011	19
2	Liverpool	1901–1990	18
3	Arsenal	1931–2004	13
4	Everton	1891–1987	9
5	Aston Villa	1894–1981	7
6	Sunderland	1892–1936	6
7	Chelsea	1955–2010	4
7	Newcastle United	1905–1927	4
7	Sheffield Wednesday	1903–1930	4

In 2010–11, United famously went top of the perch, winning their 19th league title to overhaul Liverpool's long-standing record. But what of their first success, way back in 1907–08? United started that campaign looking to build on the eighth place they had achieved in their first season back in the top flight. They got off to a stunning start, winning 13 of their first 14 games, with star striker Sandy Turnbull scoring 19 of United's 48 goals. For his performances, he received the maximum wage of just £4 per week. Of course United, as now, made full use of home advantage, but home in those days was a dilapidated stadium at Bank Street in Clayton, close to where the City of Manchester Stadium now stands. The 'advantage' was mainly due to nearby chemical works and soap factories that spewed out noxious fumes that put off all visitors. After that blistering start, United couldn't keep up the same momentum, but under the strict guidance of secretary-manager Ernest Mangnall they still eased home nine points clear of their nearest rivals, and captain Charlie Roberts lifted the league trophy for the first time.

SIR ALEX FERGUSON'S TROPHIES AT UNITED

	Competition	Winning Years	Total
1	Premier League	1993, 1994, 1996, 1997, 1999, 2000, 2001, 2003, 2007, 2008, 2009, 2011	12
2	Charity/Community Shield	1990*, 1993, 1994, 1996, 1997, 2003, 2007, 2008, 2010	9
3	FA Cup	1990, 1994, 1996, 1999, 2004	5
4	League Cup	1992, 2006, 2009, 2010	4
5	Champions League	1999, 2008	2
6	European Cup-Winners' Cup	1991	1
6	UEFA Super Cup	1991	1
6	Inter-continental Cup	1999	1
6	FIFA World Club Cup	2008	1

In a quarter of a century at Old Trafford, Sir Alex Ferguson has won a stunning 36 trophies. Since picking up his first piece of silverware back in 1990, the club has had just two seasons when it has finished with an empty trophy cabinet: 2001–02 and 2004–05 (in 1994–95 and 1997–98 it was the Charity Shield that spared any blushes). The best year was, without a doubt, 1999 when the club not only completed the Treble in May, but then followed that up by winning the Inter-continental Cup in November. This clash between the top teams in Europe and South America took place in Tokyo. Roy Keane scored the only goal of the match from close range after a superb run and cross from Ryan Giggs. Thereafter Brazilian side Palmeiras dominated, with keeper Mark Bosnich having one of his best games for the Reds. Afterwards the boss commented: 'I'm very pleased we've become the first English team to win the world championship. This is very special.'

*In 1990, the trophy was shared with Liverpool.

MOST HAT-TRICKS IN A CAREER

	Player	Career	Hat-tricks
1	Denis Law	1962–73	18
2	Jack Rowley	1937–55	12
3	**Dennis Viollet**	**1953–61**	**9**
4	Bobby Charlton	1956–73	7
5	Joe Cassidy	1893–1900	6
5	Tom Reid	1929–33	6
5	Stan Pearson	1937–53	6
5	David Herd	1961–68	6
5	Ruud van Nistelrooy	2001–06	6
10	Joe Spence	1919–33	5
10	Tommy Taylor	1953–58	5
10	Andrew Cole	1995–2001	5

Dennis Viollet was a Moss Side boy who grew up to be one of United's most lethal goalscorers of all time. A man who was determined to live life to the full, especially after the horrors of Munich, he was a crafty technician in and around the box. Many of his contemporaries thought it was an insult to his talents that he received only two England caps in his career, perhaps because his slight frame lulled some into believing he was not robust enough for international football. His first hat-trick for the club came in one of the most remarkable games in United's history – a 6–5 thriller at Stamford Bridge on 16 October 1954, where Viollet's three goals helped inflict a rare home defeat on the eventual champions. He kept on banging them in for United until Busby decided to move him on in 1961–62. Fortunately, Busby found an even more deadly inside-forward in time for the start of the next season: Denis Law.

MOST PROLIFIC GOALSCORERS★

	Player	Goals	Appearances	Strike Rate
1	Tommy Taylor	131	191	68.59
2	Ruud van Nistelrooy	150	219	68.49
3	Tom Reid	67	101	66.34
4	Dennis Viollet	179	293	61.09
5	Denis Law	237	404	58.66
6	Alex Dawson	54	93	58.06
7	Joe Cassidy	100	174	57.47
8	David Herd	145	265	54.72
9	Billy Whelan	52	98	53.06
10	Tommy Bamford	57	109	52.29

Only ten players in United's history have scored more than 50 goals at an average of better than one goal every two games. The man who tops the list, Tommy Taylor, could have gone on to even greater things had he not lost his life in the tragedy at Munich. He joined United in March 1953 from Barnsley, Matt Busby paying a record fee of £29,999 to bring him to Old Trafford (the extra pound went to the tea lady). A bubbly personality and a brave centre-forward, he was as good as anyone in the air, worked exceptionally hard for the cause, was comfortable using either foot and was hugely popular with team-mates and fans alike. Within two months of joining United, he was lining up for England and played a key role in helping his country to qualify for the 1958 World Cup. In each of his four full seasons at United, he scored more than 20 goals, with a best of 34 in the 1956–57 championship-winning side, including a hat-trick in the famous European Cup 10–0 victory over Anderlecht.

★Qualification: 50 goals; strike rate per 100 games.

DAYS WITH MOST MATCHES

	Date	Matches
1	26 December	88
2	1 January	52
3	25 December	33
4	27 December	31
5	10 April	30
6	31 March	28
6	2 April	28
6	17 April	28
6	21 April	28
6	7 September	28
6	28 December	28

One might have guessed that Boxing Day would be the date on which United have played most frequently, but what is more surprising is that Christmas Day should be so high on the list. In years gone by, there were often games on both Christmas Day and Boxing Day. That tradition died out in the 1950s, and the club hasn't had a fixture on 25 December since 1957. Then, champions United took on Luton Town in front of a crowd of 39,444, some 6,000 below the average home league gate that season. United won the game 3–0, with goals from Bobby Charlton, Duncan Edwards (a penalty) and Tommy Taylor. The Babes had been below par that season, and Busby had recently made a rare signing to strengthen his defence, recruiting Northern Ireland goalkeeper Harry Gregg from Doncaster Rovers for a world-record fee for a keeper of £23,000. This was only his second match for United, and the Reds were unbeaten in his first 15 games for the club.

BIGGEST WINS AGAINST ARSENAL

	Date	Venue	Score	Scorers
1	26 April 1952	Old Trafford	6–1	Rowley 3, Pearson 2, Byrne
1	25 February 2001	Old Trafford	6–1	Yorke 3, Keane, Sheringham, Solskjaer
3	26 December 1910	Old Trafford	5–0	Picken 2, West 2, Meredith
4	9 February 1957	Old Trafford	6–2	Whelan 2, Berry 2, Edwards, Taylor
4	28 November 1990	Highbury	6–2	Sharpe 3, Blackmore, Hughes, Wallace
6	30 November 1895	Bank Street	5–1	Cartwright 2, Clarkin, Kennedy, Peters
6	26 February 1898	Bank Street	5–1	Bryant 2, Boyd, Cassidy, Collinson
8	17 March 1984	Old Trafford	4–0	Muhren 2, Robson, Stapleton
8	16 February 2008	Old Trafford	4–0	Fletcher 2, Nani, Rooney
10	28 September 1946	Maine Road	5–2	Hanlon 2, Rowley 2, Wrigglesworth

In the last 15 years, there have been just three occasions when Arsenal have failed to join United in the top three in the Premier League. And while the rivalry between the fans doesn't have the same intensity as some of United's other opponents, the Gunners have often been the Reds' main competition in the search for domestic honours. On the pitch, this struggle for supremacy has occasionally boiled over. All of which makes the result in February 2001 particularly special. United were running away with the title, but Arsenal were their nearest challengers, hoping for an upset. Instead, Dwight Yorke had a hat-trick inside 22 minutes, Roy Keane and Ole Gunnar Solskjaer added two more goals before half-time, and former Spurs man Teddy Sheringham rounded it all off with a goal in the final minute to rub salt in the wounds. United might have been helped by injuries to the Arsenal defence, depriving them of Adams, Keown and Dixon, but it was in midfield that the Reds bossed it, with Roy Keane in magnificent form.

LONGEST CAREERS AT UNITED

	Player	Debut	Final Game	Total
1	Ryan Giggs	2 Mar 1991	28 May 2011★	20y 87d
2	Gary Neville	16 Sep 1992	1 Jan 2011	18y 107d
3	Jack Rowley	23 Oct 1937	19 Feb 1955	17y 119d
4	Paul Scholes	21 Sep 1994	28 May 2011	16y 249d
5	Bill Foulkes	13 Dec 1952	16 Aug 1969	16y 246d
6	Bobby Charlton	6 Oct 1956	28 Apr 1973	16y 204d
7	Stan Pearson	13 Nov 1937	24 Oct 1953	15y 345d
8	Johnny Carey	25 Sep 1937	25 Apr 1953	15y 212d
9	Jack Silcock	30 Aug 1919	10 Mar 1934	14y 192d
10	Billy Meredith	1 Jan 1907	7 May 1921	14y 123d

Although Gary Neville ranks only fifth on the list of most appearances for United, with 602, his career span is second only to Ryan Giggs. Neville made his debut as a substitute in the first round of the UEFA Cup against Torpedo Moscow, coming on for Lee Martin. He had already experienced trophy success for the Reds, as part of the famous Youth Cup-winning side of that year. With England international Paul Parker stationed at right-back in his early years, it wasn't until 1995–96 that he became a regular in the United line-up, winning the first of his eight titles that season and also appearing in the FA Cup final to secure the Double. He succeeded Roy Keane as United captain during the 2005–06 season, picking up the League Cup at Cardiff. After a run of injuries late in his career, he struggled to get into the side in 2010–11, and decided to call it a day midway through the campaign. He donated the proceeds from his testimonial to sustainable projects, and towards helping the fans.

★To date.

LONGEST-SERVING CURRENT UNITED PLAYERS

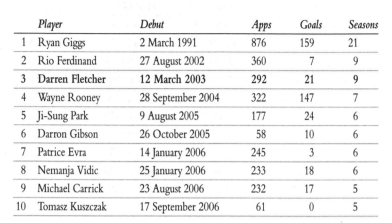

	Player	Debut	Apps	Goals	Seasons
1	Ryan Giggs	2 March 1991	876	159	21
2	Rio Ferdinand	27 August 2002	360	7	9
3	Darren Fletcher	12 March 2003	292	21	9
4	Wayne Rooney	28 September 2004	322	147	7
5	Ji-Sung Park	9 August 2005	177	24	6
6	Darron Gibson	26 October 2005	58	10	6
7	Patrice Evra	14 January 2006	245	3	6
8	Nemanja Vidic	25 January 2006	233	18	6
9	Michael Carrick	23 August 2006	232	17	5
10	Tomasz Kuszczak	17 September 2006	61	0	5

With the retirement of Gary Neville, Paul Scholes and Edwin van der Sar by the end of the 2010–11 season, and the sale of Wes Brown and John O'Shea in the summer, this list had undergone some dramatic changes in a few months. Moving up the list and reflecting his growing importance in the camp, Darren Fletcher has developed into one of United's key midfielders, helping the Reds to four league titles. He has also been unlucky, too, having missed out on all three of United's recent Champions League finals: in 2008, he was an unused substitute; the following year, he was harshly suspended; while in 2011, a mystery virus meant he wasn't sufficiently match fit for more than a place on the bench, and was again unused. Despite that, he is now a regular starter for the side in the key games, with a great ability to break up opposition attacks, as well as being able to pick out a pass to one of his own team. He may never be the flashiest of players, but he is crucial to the smooth running and success of the team.

MOST FA CUP WINS

	Team	Period	Wins
1	Manchester United	1909–2004	11
2	Arsenal	1930–2005	10
3	Tottenham Hotspur	1901–1991	8
4	Aston Villa	1887–1957	7
4	Liverpool	1965–2006	7
6	Chelsea	1970–2010	6
6	Blackburn Rovers	1884–1928	6
6	Newcastle United	1910–1955	6
9	Everton	1906–1995	5
9	Manchester City	1904–2011	5
9	The Wanderers	1872–1878	5
9	West Bromwich Albion	1888–1968	5

United have long held the record as the most successful FA Cup team in history. Their biggest wins came in 1983 (against Brighton, after a replay) and in 1994 – both by 4–0. In 1994, however, United were not up against a relegated club but against Chelsea, then under player-manager Glenn Hoddle. What's more, there was the added pressure of the chance to clinch the club's first ever Double, having already won the Premier League. For the first hour, at a rain-swept Wembley, the favourites struggled to overcome the Londoners, but then Denis Irwin was fouled in the penalty box and Eric Cantona sent his spot-kick past Dmitri Kharine. Seven minutes later, a more controversial penalty was awarded, and the Frenchman again did the business. With Chelsea now a beaten side, Mark Hughes and Brian McClair rounded off the scoring to seal a most emphatic Double.

MATT BUSBY'S MAJOR TROPHIES

	Competition	Season	Runners-up	Score
1	FA Cup	1947–48	Blackpool	4–2
2	League Championship	1951–52	Tottenham Hotspur	57pts
3	League Championship	1955–56	Blackpool	60pts
4	League Championship	1956–57	Tottenham Hotspur	64pts
5	FA Cup	1962–63	Leicester City	3–1
6	League Championship	1964–65	Leeds United	61pts
7	League Championship	1966–67	Nottingham Forest	60pts
8	European Cup	1967–68	Benfica	4–1

While the number of trophies won by Sir Matt Busby does not begin to compare with the total secured by Sir Alex Ferguson, the challenges he faced were arguably far greater. In the first instance, when he took up his position at United in October 1945, he was joining a club that had spent nine of the 20 inter-war seasons in the Second Division. Not only that, but the club had nearly gone bankrupt during that period, and hadn't won a major trophy since 1911. If that wasn't bad enough, he had the added problem that Old Trafford had been bombed during the war, so the club didn't even have a home, having to rent out City's Maine Road ground until 1949. Despite all this, he soon led the club to FA Cup glory at Wembley in 1948, beating Blackpool in what is regarded as one of the best finals of all time. He then built a new, young side – the Busby Babes – who came to dominate football in the mid-1950s, before tragedy struck at Munich on 6 February 1958. Busby, seriously injured himself, fought back and rebuilt the club, aiming to honour those who had perished, eventually securing his long-held dream of winning the European Cup in 1968.

MOST PREMIER LEAGUE GOALS IN A SEASON

	Player	Season	Appearances (Sub)	Goals
1	Cristiano Ronaldo	2007–08	31 (3)	31
2	Wayne Rooney	2009–10	32	26
3	Ruud van Nistelrooy	2002–03	33 (1)	25
4	Ruud van Nistelrooy	2001–02	29 (3)	23
5	Ruud van Nistelrooy	2005–06	28 (7)	21
6	Dwight Yorke	1999–2000	29 (3)	20
6	Ruud van Nistelrooy	2003–04	31 (1)	20
6	Dimitar Berbatov	2010–11	24 (8)	20
9	Andrew Cole	1999–2000	23 (5)	19
10	Eric Cantona	1993–94	34	18
10	Ole Gunnar Solskjaer	1996–97	25 (8)	18
10	Dwight Yorke	1998–99	32	18
10	Cristiano Ronaldo	2008–09	25 (5)	18

In 2009–10, Wayne Rooney had his most prolific season to date. Following the departures of Cristiano Ronaldo and Carlos Tevez, he immediately seized the opportunity to become the key man in United's strike force. He added new facets to his game, scoring more goals from headers in this campaign than in all his others combined to date, helped by excellent service from the flanks. In the early months of 2010, he seemed almost unstoppable, scoring 12 goals in nine appearances, including all four against Hull City on 23 January. But then he picked up an injury against Bayern Munich in the Champions League quarter-final, after which he lost some of his momentum. As United missed out on the title by a single point, it was a decisive incident in the race with Chelsea.

MOST PROLIFIC PREMIER LEAGUE GOALSCORERS★

	Player	Goals	Appearances	Strike Rate
1	Ruud van Nistelrooy	95	150	63.33
2	**Dwight Yorke**	48	96	50.00
3	Andrew Cole	93	195	47.69
4	Wayne Rooney	102	217	47.00
5	Eric Cantona	64	143	44.76
6	Dimitar Berbatov	42	95	44.21
7	Cristiano Ronaldo	84	196	42.86
8	Ole Gunnar Solskjaer	91	235	38.72
9	Louis Saha	28	86	32.56
10	Mark Hughes	35	111	31.53

Dwight Yorke is one of just two United players to have averaged a goal every two games in the Premier League to date. He joined the Reds in August 1998 for a fee of £12.6 million after nine seasons at Aston Villa. On his Old Trafford debut for United, he lined up alongside Ole Gunnar Solskjaer and each man scored twice as Charlton Athletic were thumped 4–1. With Andrew Cole and Teddy Sheringham also in the squad, Alex Ferguson had a superb range of attacking options. His most successful period came later that campaign when he hit eight goals in five games after the New Year. Having scored 18 Premier League goals in the Treble season, he did even better the following campaign, scoring 20 times (the first to do so in the league since Brian McClair in 1987–88). His form in 1999–2000 helped United to their most prolific season in the Premier League, as they scored 97 goals. After those great first two campaigns, his returns diminished and he was sold to Blackburn Rovers in 2002.

★Qualification 20 goals; strike rate goals per 100 games.

UNITED'S WORLD CUP WINNERS

	Player	Country	Year
1	Bobby Charlton	England	1966
1	Nobby Stiles	England	1966
3	Fabien Barthez	France	1998
4	Kleberson	Brazil	2002
5	Gerard Pique	Spain	2010

To date there are just five people who have played for Manchester United and played in a World Cup-winning side. Of those, just two were at United at the time they won football's greatest honour: Bobby Charlton and Nobby Stiles. Stiles was a pugnacious and combative footballer, who could play in midfield or defence. Nicknamed by his team-mates the 'Toothless Tiger', he was not only dentally challenged, but short-sighted and smaller than most defenders, but he made up for all of that with his commitment and energy. A local lad from Collyhurst, he came through the junior ranks at Old Trafford, eventually making his debut in October 1960 at 18. For more than a decade, he was at the heart of the action, freeing up the more skilful members of the team to do their best. However, one should not see him as simply a destructive force; he was able to read the game expertly and was a reliable passer of the ball. Both Matt Busby and Alf Ramsey realised his value to their teams. And when there was an outcry in the World Cup about Stiles' hard-tackling during the tournament, with the FA suggesting that Stiles ought to be omitted, Ramsey not only backed him up but threatened to resign. When he travelled to Buenos Aires for the game against Estudiantes in 1968, he was welcomed as 'El Bandido', and was eventually sent off in that controversial match. In 1971, he was sold to Middlesbrough, as injuries began to curtail his effectiveness, but he remains a true United legend.

MOST FREQUENT RUNNERS-UP
IN THE LEAGUE

	Team	Period	Runners-up
1	Manchester United	1947–2010	14
2	Liverpool	1899–2009	12
3	Aston Villa	1889–1993	10
4	Arsenal	1931–2005	8
5	Everton	1890–1986	7
6	Preston North End	1891–1958	6
7	Leeds United	1965–1972	5
7	Sunderland	1894–1935	5
7	Wolverhampton Wanderers	1938–1960	5
10	Chelsea	2005–2011	4
10	Tottenham Hotspur	1922–1963	4

United hold the record as the most frequent silver medallist in league history. One of their narrowest misses came in 1994–95 when on the final day of the season Blackburn Rovers went to Anfield with a two-point cushion over United. However, because of the Reds' better goal difference, if United won at West Ham and Blackburn failed to beat fourth-placed Liverpool, the title would return to Manchester. At half-time, that looked very unlikely: after 20 minutes Alan Shearer had given Kenny Dalglish's side the lead at his manager's old club, and ten minutes later United fell behind to Michael Hughes. Brian McClair equalised early in the second half, and then John Barnes did the same for Liverpool with 25 minutes to go – one more goal for United and they could snatch it. United piled forward, but to no avail, even when Jamie Redknapp got a late Liverpool winner. To make matters worse, United then went and lost the FA Cup final six days later to conclude a frustrating season.

MOST GOALS AS A SUBSTITUTE

	Player	Career	Appearances	Goals
1	Ole Gunnar Solskjaer	1996–2007	150	28
2	Ryan Giggs	1991–	129	10
3	Paul Scholes	1994–2011	123	9
4	**Teddy Sheringham**	**1997–2001**	**52**	**8**
4	David Beckham	1992–2003	38	8
4	Wayne Rooney	2004–	34	8
4	Javier Hernandez	2010–	18	8
8	Cristiano Ronaldo	2003–09	48	7
8	Andrew Cole	1995–2001	44	7
8	Mark Robins	1988–92	43	7
8	Ruud van Nistelrooy	2001–06	19	7

Of all the leading substitute goalscorers, none scored more vital goals coming off the bench than Ole Gunnar Solskjaer and Teddy Sheringham in the 1999 Champions League final. With both Roy Keane and Paul Scholes suspended that evening, United had struggled to establish themselves once Bayern Munich took an early lead. Feeling confident they had done enough, Bayern substituted Mario Basler and Lothar Matthaus to shore up the defence. Alex Ferguson brought on more attacking options, turning first to Sheringham midway through the second half. The former Spurs man, who had joined United two seasons earlier, was always a danger in the box. Now, he stuck out his right foot and deflected Ryan Giggs' mis-hit shot past Oliver Kahn, just after the game had gone into added time. Of course, United weren't done yet. Sheringham headed on a Beckham corner and this time it was Solskjaer who applied the finishing touch. Of all the manager's substitutions, none proved as effective as these two.

LATEST UNBEATEN START TO A SEASON

	Season	Matches Played	Date of First Defeat
1	2010–11	23	29 November
2	1991–92	16	23 October
3	1956–57	15	20 October
4	1908–09	7	17 October
5	1905–06	7	14 October
6	1895–96	5	12 October
7	1984–85	11	6 October
8	1898–99	4	1 October
9	1974–75	10	28 September
10	1997–98	10	27 September

United had their best-ever start to a season in 2010–11, when they went 23 games unbeaten. It was the first time the club had ever gone into November without having lost in any competition, and they almost made it to December. The run comprised 15 Premier League games, five in the Champions League, two in the League Cup and the Community Shield. When defeat finally came, it was a comprehensive one, as the Reds lost 4–0 at West Ham United in the quarter-finals of the League Cup. Despite this excellent run, United didn't hit the top of the table for the first time until 27 November, when they completed a stunning 7–1 victory over Blackburn Rovers that featured a Premier League record-equalling five goals from Dimitar Berbatov. Along the way, there were some late comebacks to maintain their run, most notably when United went into the last ten minutes of the Premier League game at Aston Villa 2–0 down, only to fight back with goals from Federico Macheda and Nemanja Vidic.

BEST PREMIER LEAGUE TITLES★

	Season	Games	Points	Goal Diff	Average Points
1	1999–2000	38	91	52	2.39
2	2008–09	38	90	44	2.37
3	2006–07	38	89	56	2.34
4	2007–08	38	87	58	2.29
5	1993–94	42	92	42	2.19
6	2002–03	38	83	40	2.18
7	1995–96	38	82	38	2.16
8	2000–01	38	80	48	2.11
9	2010–11	38	80	41	2.11
10	1998–99	38	79	43	2.08
11	1992–93	42	84	36	2.00
12	1996–97	38	75	32	1.97

Although United won the Premier League title with more points in the Double-winning season of 1993–94, it was in 1999–2000 that the side scored the highest average of points per game. After winning the Treble in 1999, United were even more dominant domestically the following season, winning 28 games and losing just three times (all away from Old Trafford). It was United's most prolific season in the Premier League, finishing with 97 goals (an average of 2.55 per game), as they concluded the campaign with 11 straight wins, scoring a remarkable 37 goals in the process. Dwight Yorke led the way, with 20 goals, followed by Andrew Cole (19) and Ole Gunnar Solskjaer (12). In some ways, the title race was tipped in United's favour in January when the team went to Brazil for the Club World Championship and the chasing pack all dropped points while they were away.

★According to the average number of points per game.

MOST APPEARANCES IN THE CHAMPIONS LEAGUE

	Player	Career	Appearances
1	Ryan Giggs	1991–	136
2	Paul Scholes	1994–2011	128
3	**Gary Neville**	**1992–2011**	**115**
4	David Beckham	1992–2003	81
4	Ole Gunnar Solskjaer	1996–2007	81
6	Roy Keane	1993–2005	80
7	John O'Shea	1999–2011	75
8	Rio Ferdinand	2002–	74
9	Mikael Silvestre	1999–2008	69
9	Nicky Butt	1992–2004	69

Gary Neville is one of the most experienced Champions League players from anywhere in the world. He made his debut in the tournament (when it was still known as the European Cup) in the second round at the Ali Sami Yen Stadium as United took on Galatasaray on 3 November 1993. It was one of the most intimidating places to visit, with players jostled by Turkish armed paramilitary troops and even punched by the police, while the fans warned the United squad that they were facing 'your last 48 hours'. Neville came on as a substitute for Mike Phelan and helped the Reds to keep a clean sheet, though they went out on the away-goals rule. It was the sort of hostile environment he would come to thrive on. For much of the 17 years that followed, he was United's first-choice right-back and, but for injury problems, would have made even more appearances. His highlight was being part of the United side that won the Champions League in 1999, but he missed both the 2008 and 2009 finals.

MOST APPEARANCES IN THE
PREMIER LEAGUE OVERALL

	Player	Teams	Appearances
1	Ryan Giggs	Manchester United	573
2	David James	L'pool, A Villa, West Ham, Man C, Portsmouth	572
3	Gary Speed	Leeds U, Everton, Newcastle U, Bolton W	534
4	Sol Campbell	Spurs, Arsenal, Portsmouth, Newcastle U	503
5	Frank Lampard	West Ham United, Chelsea	492
6	Emile Heskey	Leicester, L'pool, Birmingham, Wigan, A Villa	488
7	Paul Scholes	Manchester United	466
8	Jamie Carragher	Liverpool	463
9	Phil Neville	Manchester United, Everton	460
10	Alan Shearer	Blackburn Rovers, Newcastle United	441

On 15 August 1992, the Premier League era began – and Ryan Giggs was in action for United as they took on Sheffield United. Before the month was over, he had scored his first goal in the Premier League – against Nottingham Forest. Since then, he has appeared in every Premier League season, and scored in every one of them. No one else has achieved either feat. In the 19 Premier League campaigns to date, his 'worst' season (in terms of number of appearances) came in 1998–99 when he played just 24 times, while his best season was that first one, when he played 41 times. He is still some way short of being one of the Top 10 oldest outfield players in the Premier League, but if he is still playing at Christmas 2012, he will have joined that list, too. To break Teddy Sheringham's record, he will need to be turning out at the start of the 2014–15 season. Any goal he scores in 2011–12 will put him among the Top 10 oldest goalscorers.

PROGRESSION OF RECORD HOLDERS
FOR MOST APPEARANCES

	Player	Career	Gained Record	Appearances
1	Andrew Mitchell*	1886–94	9 December 1893	64
2	Willie Stewart†	1890–95	8 September 1894	87
3	George Perrins¹	1892–96	6 October 1894	102
4	Fred Erentz²	1892–1902	9 November 1895	310
5	**George Wall**	**1906–15**	**21 November 1914**	**319**
6	Billy Meredith	1907–21	26 April 1920	335
7	Joe Spence	1919–33	27 August 1928	510
8	Bill Foulkes	1952–69	11 November 1964	688
9	Bobby Charlton	1956–73	27 November 1971	758
10	Ryan Giggs	1991–	21 May 2008	876

George Wall was born in 1885 in Boldon Colliery, County Durham, and was signed by United from Barnsley at the end of the 1905–06 season as the club finally gained promotion back to the First Division. Usually deployed on the left-wing, Wall was a fiery character who took no nonsense from anyone – even if they were just watching. On 6 January 1912, having helped United to three trophies in the previous four seasons, Wall was in action at Goodison Park when he fouled an Everton player. A fan yelled abuse at him, and Wall immediately jumped into the crowd and punched the spectator. Wall, who played seven times for England, was a surprisingly prolific goalscorer for a winger, and was one of only three men before 1915 to score 100 goals for the club. He was still just 30 when football stopped for the war, but he left United to join Oldham in 1919.

*First to reach 50 appearances; †equalled then record of 64 appearances; ¹set new record at 65 appearances; ²Erentz overtook Perrins for the last time on this date, with his 96th appearance.

MOST GOALS IN A GAME

	Opposition	Venue	Date	Comp	Score	Total
1	Swindon Town	Stamford Bridge	25 Sep 1911	CS	8–4	12
2	Wolverhampton W	North Road	15 Oct 1892	Div 2	10–1	11
2	Liverpool	Anfield	25 Mar 1908	Div 1	4–7	11
2	Newcastle United	Old Trafford	13 Sep 1930	Div 1	4–7	11
2	Chelsea	Stamford Bridge	16 Oct 1954	Div 1	6–5	11
6	Lincoln City	Bank Street	16 Nov 1895	Div 2	5–5	10
6	Grimsby Town	Blundell Park	26 Dec 1933	Div 2	3–7	10
6	Aston Villa	Villa Park	10 Jan 1948	FAC 3	6–4	10
6	Anderlecht	Maine Road	12 Sep 1956	ECP	10–0	10
6	Newcastle United	St James' Park	2 Jan 1960	Div 1	3–7	10
6	Northampton Town	County Ground	7 Feb 1970	FAC 5	8–2	10

Having been the inaugural winners of the Charity Shield in 1908, on United's second appearance in 1911 they dished up an astonishing game – and set a record yet to be equalled. To look at the scoreline, one might think it was treated as an exhibition match, but according to F.B. Wilson of the *Daily Mirror* that would be the view of 'the man who merely read, but did not watch'. Southern League Swindon took an early advantage when United skipper Charlie Roberts was off the pitch to score after six minutes. But United hit back with goals from Sandy Turnbull and a hat-trick from Harold Halse (though the man from the *Mirror* credited one of them to Mickey Hamill), as United went into the interval 4–3 up. The second half was a masterclass from Halse, who added another three goals to take his tally to six. His fourth 'was a pretty goal', as the Swindon defender bought his dummy, while his fifth was 'an extraordinary screw kick'.

FA CUP WINS

	Opponent	Date	Result	Scorers
1	Bristol City	24 April 1909	1–0	A. Turnbull
2	Blackpool	24 April 1948	4–2	Rowley 2, Anderson, Pearson
3	Leicester City	25 May 1963	3–1	Herd 2, Law
4	Liverpool	21 May 1977	2–1	J. Greenhoff, Pearson
5	Brighton & Hove A	26 May 1983	4–0*	Robson 2, Muhren, Whiteside
6	Everton	18 May 1985	1–0	Whiteside
7	Crystal Palace	17 May 1990	1–0*	Martin
8	Chelsea	14 May 1994	4–0	Cantona 2, Hughes, McClair
9	Liverpool	11 May 1996	1–0	Cantona
10	Newcastle United	22 May 1999	2–0	Scholes, Sheringham
11	Millwall	22 May 2004	3–0	Van Nistelrooy 2, Ronaldo

United hold the record for most FA Cup wins (11), just ahead of Arsenal (10). While many hold the 1948 final, when United beat a Matthews-inspired Blackpool to take the trophy, to have been one of the best ever, few would say the same of the 1996 final. However, it was one of the most significant of all United's wins. That season, Eric Cantona had returned from a nine-month ban for his attack on a fan at Selhurst Park in January 1995. As captain, he inspired his young side (including relative novices such as David Beckham, Nicky Butt, Gary and Phil Neville and Paul Scholes) on their run to Wembley. He scored in every round bar the semi-final. And on the big occasion itself, when Liverpool famously took a walk round the pitch in cream suits, he found a stunning late finish – volleying in from the edge of the box – to win the trophy, complete the Double and fully justify why he was FWA Footballer of the Year.

*Score in the replay.

EUROPEAN FINALS

	Opposition	Competition	Date	Venue	Score
1	Benfica	European Cup	29 May 1968	Wembley	4–1
2	Barcelona	European Cup-Winners' Cup	15 May 1991	Rotterdam	2–1
3	Red Star Belgrade	Super Cup	19 Nov 1991	Old Trafford	1–0
4	Bayern Munich	Champions League	26 May 1999	Barcelona	2–1
5	Lazio	Super Cup	27 Aug 1999	Monaco	0–1
6	Chelsea	Champions League	21 May 2008	Moscow	1–1*
7	Zenit St Petersburg	Super Cup	29 Aug 2008	Monaco	1–2
8	Barcelona	Champions League	27 May 2009	Rome	0–2
9	Barcelona	Champions League	28 May 2011	Wembley	1–3

United's first European final was surely the most intense and emotional of them all. Having been the English pioneers of European football back in 1956–57, United's attempts to become European champions had been dealt a devastating blow by the Munich Air Disaster of 6 February 1958. A decade on, Matt Busby finally had the chance to honour those who had died in Germany by winning the trophy he had dreamed of. Two Munich survivors formed part of the team that hot night at Wembley: Bobby Charlton and Bill Foulkes. Appropriately enough, it was the former who gave United the lead early in the second half, heading home David Sadler's cross from eight yards out. But Benfica equalised and the game went to extra time. George Best and Brian Kidd both scored, but Charlton had the final word when he added a fourth from Kidd's pass. Busby said afterwards: 'It eased the pain of the guilt of going into Europe. It was my justification.' Meanwhile, Charlton was so overcome by exhaustion that when he got back to the club hotel he fainted several times and missed the celebrations.

*United won the penalty shootout 6–5.

MOST GOALS SCORED IN A SEASON

	Player	Season	Appearances (Sub)	Goals
1	Denis Law	1963–64	42	46
2	Ruud van Nistelrooy	2002–03	50 (2)	44
3	Cristiano Ronaldo	2007–08	46 (3)	42
4	Denis Law	1964–65	52	39
5	Ruud van Nistelrooy	2001–02	44 (5)	36
6	Tommy Taylor	1956–57	45	34
6	Wayne Rooney	2009–10	42 (2)	34
8	Billy Whelan	1956–57	54	33
8	David Herd	1965–66	51 (1)	33
10	Dennis Viollet	1959–60	39	32
10	George Best	1967–68	53	32

Denis Law's extraordinary instinct for goal is clearly shown by the list above. Along with Ruud van Nistelrooy, he is one of only two men to appear twice. He joined United on 10 July 1962 for a record fee of £115,000. At the time, United still had not fully recovered from the Munich disaster and many of the players brought in to replace the fallen legends had struggled to live up to the impossible expectations put upon them. Law wasn't going to be intimidated by that, or his price tag. A supreme poacher of goals, he was combative, fearless and deadly; the Old Trafford crowd took to him instantly, dubbing him 'The King'. After an excellent first campaign, when he scored 29 goals, in his second season he was even better. He was unstoppable, scoring an astonishing seven hat-tricks in 1963–64, and was named European Footballer of the Year for his efforts. It wasn't quite enough to win any trophies, but that was put right the following season when United won the league title.

MOST RECENT RECRUITS

	Player	From	Date	Apps (Goals)
1	David De Gea	Atletico Madrid	29 June 2011	0
2	Ashley Young	Aston Villa	23 June 2011	0
3	Phil Jones	Blackburn Rovers	13 June 2011	0
4	Anders Lindegaard	Aalesund	4 January 2011	2
5	Bébé	Vitoria de Guimaraes	4 August 2010	7 (2)
6	Chris Smalling	Fulham	7 July 2010	33 (1)
7	Javier Hernandez	Chivas de Guadalajara	1 July 2010	45 (20)
8	Mame Biram Diouf	Molde	30 July 2009	6 (1)
9	Gabriel Obertan★	Bordeaux	8 July 2009	28 (1)
10	Michael Owen	Newcastle United	3 July 2009	48 (14)
11	Antonio Valencia	Wigan Athletic	30 June 2009	69 (10)

Over the last two years, Sir Alex Ferguson has brought in an entire new team as he continues to build for the future. The summer of 2011 saw him spending more than in recent years as he signed up three new recruits for a combined fee of about £50 million. Phil Jones, the 19-year-old Preston-born England Under-21 defender, had made his league debut for Blackburn in March 2010, and quickly became one of the most highly rated young defenders in the country. Ashley Young celebrated his 26th birthday a few days after joining the Reds. The exciting forward, who can play on the wing or as a support striker, had joined Aston Villa in the January transfer window in 2007 and soon after made his England debut. Finally, David De Gea was brought in to replace Edwin van der Sar. The Spanish Under-21 keeper had made his La Liga debut in October 2009, just before his 19th birthday, and quickly established himself as Atletico's No 1.

★He was sold to Newcastle United in August 2011.

LAST-MINUTE GOALS

	Opposition	Date	Competition	Score	Scorer
1	Liverpool	6 March 2011	PL	1–3	Hernandez
2	Wolverhampton W	6 November 2010	PL	2–1	Ji-sung Park
3	Wolverhampton W	26 October 2010	LC 4	3–2	Hernandez
4	Chelsea	8 August 2010	CS	3–1	Berbatov
5	Manchester City	17 April 2010	PL	1–0	Scholes
6	Manchester City	27 January 2010	LC SF 2nd	3–1	Rooney
7	Hull City	23 January 2010	PL	4–0	Rooney
8	Burnley	16 January 2010	PL	3–0	Diouf
9	Wolfsburg	8 December 2009	CL Gp	3–1	Owen
10	CSKA Moscow	3 November 2009	CL Gp	3–3	Valencia
11	Sunderland	3 October 2009	PL	2–2	Own goal
12	**Manchester City**	**20 September 2009**	**PL**	**4–3**	**Owen**
13	Wigan Athletic	22 August 2009	PL	5–0	Nani
14	Chelsea	9 August 2009	CS	2–2	Rooney

In the last two seasons, United have scored 14 goals in the last minute. But the game that stands out most of all is the Premier League derby-day thriller at Old Trafford in September 2009. With neighbours City newly awash with cash, they were looking to show they were the best team in Manchester. United had a point to prove from the start: Wayne Rooney scored first, but City equalised; early in the second half Darren Fletcher put the Reds back in front, only for the Blues to peg them back. Late on, Fletcher scored a seemingly decisive goal, but still City drew level. Finally, in the 96th minute, Ryan Giggs played the perfect pass to Michael Owen to hit home. Exhilarating!

THE ALL-TIME TOP 10 GREATEST UNITED
PLAYERS AS VOTED BY THE FANS

	Player	Career	Appearances	Goals
1	Ryan Giggs	1991–	876	159
2	Eric Cantona	1992–97	185	82
3	George Best	1963–74	470	179
4	Bobby Charlton	1956–73	758	249
5	Cristiano Ronaldo	2003–09	292	118
6	Paul Scholes	1994–2011	676	150
7	David Beckham	1993–2003	394	85
8	Roy Keane	1993–2005	480	51
9	Peter Schmeichel	1991–99	398	1
10	Wayne Rooney	2004–	322	147

In 2011, *Inside United* magazine and manutd.com asked fans to vote for their three all-time greatest players and this list was the result. Duncan Edwards, Ole Gunnar Solskjaer, Denis Law, Bryan Robson and Ruud van Nistelrooy filled the next five positions. That Giggs came top is a reflection of the huge admiration felt for a player who continues to set new standards on the pitch. In April 2011, he even found himself filling in as an attacking left-back against West Ham and winning Sky's Man of the Match award. As Sir Alex Ferguson commented: 'When you look at the galaxy of stars that have been at this club, this is a huge honour for Ryan.' Giggs added: 'I couldn't believe it, to be honest.' His own vote went to those he had played alongside, Schmeichel, Keane and Scholes, who was top of his list. Steve Bruce, who played alongside Giggs on the day he made his starting debut, against Manchester City on 4 May 1991, said: 'Ryan has to be the greatest ever to have played in the Premier League.'

INDEX OF PERSONS

Djemba-Djemba, Eric 137
Djordjic, Bojan 91
Docherty, Tommy 59, 65, 135, 150
Doherty, John 120
Donaghy, Mal 82
Donaldson, Bob 17, 40, 130
Dong Fangzhuo 137
Doughty, Jack 79
Doughty, Roger 79
Downie, John 160
Dublin, Dion 33, 37, 86, 111
Duckworth, Dick 96
Duncan, Scott 135, 150
Dunne, Pat 93
Dunne, Tony 13, 19, 20, 26, 72, 88, 93, 149
Duxbury, Mike 60, 64, 149

Eagles, Chris 29
Ebanks-Blake, Sylvan 29, 105, 119
Eckersley, Adam 97
Eckersley, Richard 97, 105
Edwards, Duncan 69, 120, 134
Erentz, Fred 16, 40, 109, 181
Evans, Jonny 82
Evra, Patrice 18, 34, 51, 55, 62, 138, 169

Farman, Alf 40
Ferdinand, Rio 18, 78, 102, 159, 169, 179
Ferguson, Sir Alex 57, 94, 123, 135, 150, 159, 163
Ferguson, Darren 41, 118
Fitzpatrick, John 23
Fletcher, Darren 16, 55, 62, 104, 105, 169
Forlan, Diego 50, 54, 71, 104
Forsyth, Alex 59, 65
Fortune, Quinton 50, 137
Foster, Ben 119
Foulkes, Bill 13, 26, 72, 93, 149, 152, 168, 181

Gaskell, David 120
Gibson, Colin 75, 116
Gibson, Darron 67, 75, 169

Gibson, Don 75, 82
Gibson, Richard 75
Gibson, Terry 75
Gidman, John 112, 116
Giggs, Ryan 41, 49, 128, 136, 168, 169, 188; appearances 13, 26, 31, 52, 60, 83, 98, 104, 179, 180, 181; goals 14, 30, 33, 53, 61, 131, 176
Gill, Oliver 105
Goram, Andy 48, 101
Graham, George 65, 122
Greenhoff, Jimmy 59
Greening, Jonathan 119
Gregg, Harry 20, 69, 80, 90
Griffiths, Jack 19
Grimes, Ashley 59

Halse, Harold 79, 96
Hamill, Mickey 79
Hardman, Harold 48
Haroun, Denzil 105
Hayes, Vince 96
Heinze, Gabriel 71, 142
Henry, Thierry 31
Herd, David 17, 20, 23, 73, 93, 99, 117, 143, 164, 165, 185
Hernandez, Javier 50, 55, 62, 71, 142, 176, 186, 187
Heskey, Emile 180
Hilditch, Clarence 109
Hill, Gordon 59
Hogg, Graeme 19
Holden, Dick 82
Holton, Jim 59, 65
Houston, Stewart 59, 65, 111
Howard, Tim 101, 119
Hughes, Mark 41, 86, 118, 123, 128; appearances 26, 52, 60; goals 33, 53, 61, 131, 143, 173

Ince, Paul 33, 41, 78, 86, 118, 123
Irwin, Denis 41, 136; appearances 13, 60, 88, 98, 26, 138, 149, 159; goals 33, 89

Jackson, Bill 53

James, David 180
Jenkyns, Caesar 79
Jones, David (1937) 75
Jones, David (2004) 75, 105
Jones, Mark 19, 75, 120, 134
Jones, Owen 75
Jones, Peter 75
Jones, Phil 186
Jones, Richard ('Richie') 75, 97
Jones, Tom 52, 75, 82
Jones, Tommy 75
Jordan, Joe 21, 84, 111
Jovanovic, Nikola 84, 91, 110

Kanchelskis, Andrei 33, 35, 41, 86, 91, 110, 112, 154
Keane, Roy 32, 37, 118, 128, 136, 188; appearances 26, 88, 98, 159, 179; goals 30, 89
Keane, Will 67
Kendall, Howard 122
Kidd, Brian 61, 94, 112, 141
Kinsey, Albert 29
Kleberson 71, 174
Knox, Archie 94
Kuszczak, Tomasz 91, 169

Lambert, Paul 57
Lampard, Frank 180
Lancaster, Joe 111
Larsson, Henrik 37
Law, Denis 69, 112; appearances 16, 20, 26; goals 17, 27, 30, 73, 99, 114, 117, 131, 143, 164, 165, 185
Lee, Kieran 105
Lewis, Billy 140
Lewis, Eddie 120
Lindegaard, Anders 186
Lucio 18
Lyall, John 122
Lynch, Mark 97
Lynn, Sammy 160

Macari, Lou 16, 17, 37, 59, 61, 65
McCalliog, Jim 65
McCarthy, Mick 57

McClair, Brian 37, 41, 123; appearances 16, 26, 54, 60, 104, 126, 138, 159; goals 17, 33, 61, 143
McClaren, Steve 94
McCreery, David 54, 104
McGrath, Paul 116
McGuinness, Wilf 120
Macheda, Federico 67
McIlroy, Sammy 49, 88, 89, 112, 118, 126
McIlvenny, Eddie 110
McQueen, Gordon 84
McShane, Harry 48
Maicon 18
Maldini, Paolo 31
Mancini, Roberto 57
Mangnall, Ernest 135, 150
Manley, Tom 49
Manucho 137
Martin, Lee 37, 123
Martinez, Roberto 57
Mathieson, William 40
Mellor, Jack 82
Meredith, Billy 49, 52, 53, 79, 96, 109, 140, 168, 181
Mew, Jack 80
Miller, Liam 37
Milne, Robert 140
Mitchell, Andrew 181
Mitten, Charlie 126, 137, 160
Moger, Harry 80, 96
Moore, Charlie 82, 109
Moore, John 122
Moran, Kevin 84, 88, 89
Morgan, Willie 16, 20
Morris, Charlie 140
Morrison, Ravel 97
Moses, Remi 116
Moyes, David 57
Muhren, Arnold 110, 116
Murphy, Jimmy 67

Nani 35, 55, 62, 187
Nesta, Alessandro 18
Neville, Gary 13, 26, 31, 64, 74, 98, 102, 136, 152, 168, 179

Neville, Phil 64, 98, 102, 104, 119, 136, 180
Nevland, Erik 29

Obertan, Gabriel 51, 186
Olive, Les 48
Olsen, Jesper 110, 116
O'Shea, John 54, 62, 88, 98, 104, 105, 179
Owen, Bill 75
Owen, George 75, 79
Owen, Jack 75, 79
Owen, Michael 54, 75, 78, 99, 186, 187
Owen, W. 75

Pallister, Gary 41, 60, 86, 123, 128, 138, 149, 152, 159
Park Ji-Sung 34, 50, 137, 169, 187
Parker, Paul 86
Paterson, Steve 65
Pearson, Stan 27, 73, 143, 153, 160, 164, 168
Pearson, Stuart 59
Peddie, Jack 17
Pegg, David 120, 134
Perrins, George 40, 82, 181
Phelan, Mike 94, 123, 138
Picken, Jack 117
Pique, Gerard 174
Pleat, David 122
Poborsky, Karel 91
Pogba, Paul 51
Powell, Jack 79
Preston, Stephen 111
Prunier, William 51
Pugh, Danny 97
Pulis, Tony 57
Puyol, Carles 18

Queiroz, Carlos 94

Rachubka, Paul 101
Raul 31
Redknapp, Harry 57
Reid, Tom 17, 164, 165
Ricardo 101
Richardson, Kieran 64

Roberto Carlos 18, 31
Roberts, Charlie 79, 96, 109
Robins, Mark 118, 176
Robson, Bryan 21, 49, 60, 69, 72, 78, 86, 102, 116, 123, 152
Robson, John 135
Ronaldo, Cristiano 32, 34, 128, 142, 188; goals 14, 30, 35, 50, 114, 141, 143, 172, 173, 176, 185
Rooney, Wayne 32, 55, 78, 128, 142, 169, 188; appearances 62, 102, 159; goals 14, 30, 99, 114, 141, 153, 172, 173, 176, 185, 187
Rossi, Giuseppe 67, 105
Roughton, George 82
Rowley, Jack 160, 168; appearances 72, 152; goals 27, 73, 114, 117, 130, 131, 143, 153, 164
Ryan, Jim ('Jimmy') 23, 94

Sadler, David 20, 23
Saha, Louis 35, 51, 61, 173
Sartori, Carlo 110
Schmeichel, Peter 29, 41, 110, 112, 188; appearances 34, 80, 98, 126, 138, 149, 159
Scholes, Paul 64, 136, 168, 188; appearances 13, 31, 62, 98, 102, 104, 152, 179, 180; goals 14, 30, 50, 61, 131, 143, 153, 154, 176, 187
Scott, Billy 140
Sealey, Les 123
Seedorf, Clarence 31
Sexton, Dave 84, 150
Sharpe, Lee 33, 61
Shawcross, Ryan 119
Shearer, Alan 180
Sheringham, Teddy 32, 54, 128, 141, 154, 176
Shevchenko, Andriy 31
Sidebottom, Arnold 48